FAITH ON EARTH

AN INQUIRY INTO

THE STRUCTURE OF

HUMAN FAITH

BY H. RICHARD NIEBUHR

EDITED BY

RICHARD R. NIEBUHR

Faith

YALE UNIVERSITY PRESS

on

NEW HAVEN & LONDON

Earth

Designed by Richard Hendel
and set in Sabon type
by Tseng Information Systems, Inc.
Printed in the United States of America.

Library of Congress
Cataloging-in-Publication Data
Niebuhr, H. Richard (Helmut Richard),
1894–1962.
    Faith on earth : an inquiry into the structure
    of human faith / H. Richard Niebuhr ; edited
    by Richard R. Niebuhr.
        p.   cm.
    Includes index.
    ISBN 0–300–04315–5 (alk. paper)
    1. Faith.   I. Niebuhr, Richard R.   II. Title.
    BT771.2.N54   1989   89–30178
    234'.2—dc 19   CIP

10 9 8 7 6 5 4 3 2 1

To the memory of

CYNTHIA M. NIEBUHR

1922–1979

RRN

CONTENTS

PREFACE

"When the Son of man comes, will he find faith on earth?" H. Richard Niebuhr (HRN) spent years exploring substantive issues that this question attracts to itself, much as a magnet attracts susceptible particles into its field of energy. He explored not to locate the question's early significance in the Gospel according to Luke or to speculate on end-times but to inquire into the forms and structure of human faith as we experience faith in our times and thus into the nature of our social selfhood. While his other books give evidence of the breadth and of the many perspectives of his inquiry into faith, *Faith on Earth* is the most personal of all these—it conducts us farther and deeper into the author's understanding of the fiducial constitution of our existence as loyal-disloyal beings who keep faith and break faith.

Some who have read these pages in manuscript form have characterized *Faith on Earth* as a phenomenology of faith. That characterization strikes me as fair enough; at least I do not know what else to offer in its place. But if this book is a phenomenology it is of a different kind than recent philosophical phenomenology or phenomenology of religion. For some it may bring to mind the protophenomenology of William James's *Principles of Psychology* and for others the semiotic and associated phenomenology of C. S. Peirce, as mediated through Josiah Royce. (I have encountered no evidence, however, that the author read Peirce, though James's work he knew and Royce's he knew well.) But ticketing and labeling the method and contents of this book is not my foremost concern as editor. It is clear that the author proceeded by *reflection*, by tactful *description*, and by careful *analysis*. This procedure carried him to places in our interpersonal existence where the psychological, moral, and religious energies of our social worlds converge in our dispositions to trust and distrust, in our attitudes of believing and disbelieving, and in our acts of loyalty and disloyalty.

Preparation of the Text

The text of *Faith on Earth* principally depends on three internally related sources, identified in the Table of Manuscripts. The first and largest of these is a manuscript bearing the title "On Faith," which is described in item 4 of the table. Directly associated with this book length manuscript is a revised version of chapter 1 of "On Faith" (item 4c of the table), and it is from this source that the title "Faith on Earth: An Inquiry into the Structure of Human Faith" derives. Item 5 in the table, "The Method of Reflection," has been incorporated into the edited text of *Faith on Earth* as chapter 2, the place for which the author apparently originally intended it but from which at some undetermined time he removed it. This chapter is unfinished; nonetheless, since to my knowledge it is the best statement by HRN on his mode of thinking about faith, I have thought it justifiable to include it, especially since the entire work is cast in the very mode of reflection that this chapter sets forth. Similarly, chapter 7, "The Community of Faith," is apparently unfinished. The final paragraphs in this chapter point toward topics the author evidently intended to take up but in fact did not in this manuscript. Readers may turn to *Radical Monotheism and Western Culture* and the essays appended in that book to find the author addressing such issues as he apparently had in mind here.

A supporting manuscript source is the collection in five folders of materials identified by the author as the Stone Lectures and entitled "Knowledge of Faith." These lectures are almost immediately antecedent to the manuscript "On Faith" and have been substantially incorporated into it. Since some of the typing in "On Faith" was done by another hand, I have used the Stone Lectures to verify the typescript of "On Faith," to rectify uncorrected slips and misreadings of HRN's handwritten revisions and marginal notes, and to supply clues for completing minor stylistic revisions that HRN left unfinished. The Stone Lectures, in turn, were preceded by another set on the same topic, the Swander Lectures, and the latter in turn by an earlier manuscript of four typed chapters.

These materials and all the other items listed in the Table of Manuscripts are lodged in the Andover-Harvard Theological Library of the Harvard Divinity School.

For the most part I have left the punctuation alone, even though it is spare, but in some instances I have changed it in minor ways. Capitalization has posed a special problem, since it is irregular in the manuscripts; again, I have modified it only slightly. Brackets in the text indicate deletions by the author that I have restored. The edited text remains less polished than, one supposes, the author would have liked. I have supplied a fair number of editorial notes, mainly for the purpose of completing references within the manuscript materials, which the author indicated but left unfinished. For this purpose, wherever possible I have made use of books remaining from his own library, books that in many instances bear his own underlinings and marginal notations. As a consequence of this editorial procedure, the references to other literature are for the greater part to the editions the author himself used. In a few instances, having no clues to follow, I have cited more recent editions. In one or two cases, I have substituted the language of now standard translations for that of older translations that the author quoted.

It is difficult to determine at precisely what time the author began the work represented here. The four-chapter manuscript "Knowledge of Faith," item 1 in the Table of Manuscripts, provides a clue that the time was the mid-1940s. But still other papers, not listed here, suggest that his serious reflections on the themes of this book commenced much earlier. One bit of internal evidence indicates that HRN was still occupied with this project in 1958, namely, the reference to Michael Polanyi's *Personal Knowledge* penciled at the bottom of page 2 of the last known revision of the first chapter of the main manuscript (item 4c in the table). Hence, *Faith on Earth* bears witness to a concern utterly central to the author during the 1940s and 1950s. Readers who recall those decades, the onset of the Cold War, the Korean War, and the reckless persecution of many Americans as unpatriotic and traitorous, spearheaded by Senator Joseph McCarthy of Wisconsin, will recognize the background against which the author carried on his reflections. But these public events scarcely exhaust all that was in HRN's mind and heart as he composed his thinking about faith on earth.

As I pursued my editorial work, the television networks and the newspapers were carrying their reportage of the congressional "Iran-*contra* Hearings." The appalling public testimony of some of the persons summoned before the joint House and Senate committees conducting those hearings, as well as the equivocal silence and contradictory statements of others centrally concerned, sounded as a sad and ominous counterpoint to the sentences and paragraphs I was then contemplating and underscored the weight of the analyses contained in the chapters "Believing and Knowing in Community," "The Structure of Faith," and "Broken Faith."

Why HRN did not bring this long-standing project to publication must remain a matter of conjecture. There is, of course, the fact that he carried many other heavy obligations in the years he worked on this book. Among these, during the 1950s, were his responsibilities, in association with James M. Gustafson and the late Daniel Day Williams, for the Study of Theological Education in the United States and Canada commissioned by the American Association of Theological Schools.

It may be helpful to place *Faith on Earth* in relation to immediately preceding and succeeding books: *The Meaning of Revelation*, 1941; *Christ and Culture*, 1950; *The Purpose of the Church and Its Ministry: Reflections on the Aims of Theological Education*, in collaboration with Daniel Day Williams and James M. Gustafson, 1956; *The Ministry in Historical Perspectives*, edited with Daniel Day Williams, 1956; *The Advancement of Theological Education*, written with Daniel Day Williams and James M. Gustafson, 1957; *Radical Monotheism and Western Culture*, 1960; and *The Responsible Self*, 1963 (published posthumously and edited by James M. Gustafson and Richard R. Niebuhr). *Faith on Earth* is most directly connected to *The Meaning of Revelation*, *Radical Monotheism*, and *The Responsible Self*, which remain in print more than a quarter century since their author's death.

I AM especially pleased that Yale University Press is publishing *Faith on Earth*, since H. Richard Niebuhr taught generations of students at Yale from 1931 to 1962; the enthusiasm of Charles Grench, Executive Editor, for the contents of this work greatly encouraged me in my labors. I owe much to Ronald F. Thiemann, Dean of the Harvard Divinity School, for his several decisive initiatives without which this manuscript would not have come into print. I am likewise indebted to the Lilly Endowment for the support that enabled me to take the extensive time required to do this painstaking editorial work. The knowledge of the deep interest and readiness to help on the part of my friends Hans Frei, now deceased but gratefully remembered, and James Gustafson sustained me innumerable times when I despaired that this task exceeded my capacities.

Richard R. Niebuhr

1

FAITH IN QUESTION

Questions about *faith* arise in every area of human existence. Though the word seems to be primarily religious, so that it is associated with such other terms as God, church and creed, we also use it, with its synonyms and antonyms, in many other connections. We adjure each other to have faith in democracy or in the people or in the scientific method or that right makes might. We speak of "keeping faith" with those who have died in our nation's wars; we honor men of "good faith"; we contrast the faith of democracy with the creeds of totalitarianism. Questions about faith arise in an urgent and tragic form as we view massive and petty breaches of faith—treasons, lying propaganda, the cultivation of mutual distrust as measures of party and national policy, the use of pretended loyalty in conspiracies against state and civilization, the enlistment of men as faithful followers of causes that depend for success on practices of deception. [In this situation a dark prospect opens before us as we reflect on the meaning of Jesus' question: "When the Son of man comes will he find faith on earth?" (Luke 18:8). He may have meant, "Will he find belief or trust in God?" But he may also have meant, "Will he find any faithfulness among men?"] The experiences of the twentieth century have brought into view the abyss of "faithlessness" into which men can fall. [We see this possibility—that human history will come to its end neither in a brotherhood of man nor in universal death under the blows of natural or man-made catastrophe, but in the gangrenous corruption of a social life in which every promise, contract, treaty and "word of honor" is given and accepted in deception and distrust. If men no longer have faith in each other, can they exist as men?]

Such questions about man's faith are closely connected with others about the relations of this interpersonal faith to faith in God. Political orators, often sincerely but sometimes, it seems, for the sake of gaining the support of religious people, intimately associate reliance on Deity with the maintenance of an inherited structure of human relations. They discover logical or psychological connections between the atheism of Communism and the perversion of moral integrity that marks its theory and practice. Theologians and leaders of the churches have been quick to point out these same relations. Yet other men of evident integrity as well as intelligence make a sharp distinction between the religious beliefs of the Western world and its faith in the so-called democratic practices or its loyalty to human values. With John Dewey they define and maintain loyalty to a "common faith" divorced from religious creed. With Bertrand Russell they associate religious faith with superstition and with the faithless practices of power-seeking ecclesiastical groups. Other questions about faith, similar to those that are raised in the political realm, are widely discussed in debates about the foundations of science and education. In these instances, to be sure, the word *faith* is more generally used in its meaning of "ultimate belief" than in the sense of fidelity or faithfulness. But the "fiduciary" element in science also comes up for investigation.[1] In any case among the questions asked are these: whether the knowledge that we seek to gain and to transmit is dependent in any way on ultimate beliefs about the nature of the world and the destiny of man, that is, on beliefs of a more or less religious order; whether education in the western world loses all unity when the traditional ultimate beliefs that appeared to give it some integrity in the past are abandoned; whether the moral values of democratic culture can be mediated to new generations without the religious faith with which they have been historically associated.

What faith means; what the relations of belief in God to human loyalty are; what confidence may be placed in man, or in his institutions, in Scriptures, reason, church or private intuition; how confidence is related to fidelity—these questions are raised most frequently in the conversations of specifically religious communities. They are heard there in the challenges to religious faith made by unbelievers, when

1. See Michael Polanyi's remarkable examination of the fiduciary element in science in *Personal Knowledge: Towards a Post-Critical Philosophy* (Chicago: University of Chicago Press, 1958), chapter 10 especially.

they unite with unbelief the practice of faithlessness among men, or, more seriously, when they combine unbelief in God with a high degree of social and moral fidelity. Such challenges to faith echo through all centuries. They were heard by the Hebrew poet who was distressed by those people who continually said to him, "Where is now thy God?" and no believer has been able to escape them since. From Celsus to Nietzsche and beyond they have goaded the Christian believer to try to understand and to give an account of his faith. He is prompted to do so partly, no doubt, by desire to defend himself, but partly also because he senses the presence of great confusion among his assailants [as well as in the world at large] and seeks to contribute something to their peace as well as to his own.

Problems of faith are also acute in the internal conflicts of the religious believer. He wonders at his own ability to say, "Our Father, who art in heaven," in the midst of experiences that are apparently indicative of everything else than of the presence of beneficent solicitude at the center of existence. He confesses, "I believe; help thou mine unbelief" (Mark 9:24).[2] He is bewildered by the combination of his faith with his massive unbelief. With Tolstoy's peasant he answers—at least to himself—the question whether he believes in God with the rejoinder, "No, I do not believe; for how should a man such as I am, with his anxieties and pride, with his sins and vices, be a believer in God?"[3] With Kierkegaard he notes the tension between his reasoning and his believing and with Pascal appeals paradoxically to the reasons of the heart of which reason does not know. What is the structure and character of this strange, many-faceted religious faith? How is it related

2. The author habitually used the Authorized (King James) translation of this verse. On Bible translations employed in this book, see note 23 below. [Editor's note.]

3. This is the author's paraphrase of a passage in Tolstoy's "An Appeal to the Clergy," which reads as follows: "An illiterate Samara peasant of my acquaintance in reply to the question whether he believed in God, simply and firmly replied, as his priest told me: 'No, sinner that I am, I don't believe.' He explained his disbelief in God by saying that one could not live as he was living if one believed in God: 'A man scolds, and grudges help to a beggar, and envies, and over-eats, and drinks strong drinks. Could he do such things if he believed in God?'" (Leo Tolstoy, *On Life and Essays on Religion*, trans. Aylmer Maude [London: Oxford University Press, Humphrey Milford, n.d.], 299). [Editor's note.]

to reason and to conduct? How has it entered into life and how is it maintained? Such questions are even more acute than those others that also arise in the religious realm when believers challenge each other to relate their faith to their works, to accept some version of the creed as "the true faith," or to abandon reliance upon some common belief while they seek a personal faith-relation to the ground of their being.

These many questions about faith seem to be highly heterogeneous. We are not dealing, it may appear, with one complex of interrelated problems concerning an integral element in human experience, but are rather simply following the meandering route of a stream of consciousness as we proceed by means of a process of association from one set of difficulties or debates to another. Is not the word faith so highly equivocal or even indeterminate in meaning that it cannot be significantly used in such various connections in the course of one conversation? Now it means belief in a doctrine; now the acceptance of intuited or self-evident truths; now confidence or trust; now piety in general or a historic religion. In some cases the word applies to man's relation to the supernatural but again it refers to human interpersonal relations. Do not these meanings vary so greatly that it is an illusion to think of all these faiths as having anything in common that can be a fit subject for inquiry? It may be so. It may be that the visual or auditory sign faith represents not one word but several, pointing to various unrelated things or concepts, as the sign "organ" means in one context musical instrument, in another, a part of a body, and still another, a newspaper. But it may also be that faith points to a complex structure of which now this, now that, element is focused in the attention while the remainder of the structure is implied. It may be a word like *reason,* which, equally various in its uses, yet seems to indicate a single complex process of perception and conception, distinction and comparison, experience and abstraction, intuition and inference, action and contemplation. Whether or not this is so only an inquiry, not into the uses of the word, but into some of the experiences to which the word points, can bring to light. Should it appear that believing a proposition is intimately connected with trusting a person, that trust and fidelity are inseparable, that trust in God and interpersonal faithfulness are closely associated, then it might also be indicated that there is a structure of faith, while the stresses and strains in that structure might also be brought into view. On such an inquiry we embark, not

in the hope of being able to map the world of faith but with the desire
to understand, albeit roughly and in outline, the relations of some of
its continents and seas.

S o m e preliminary orientation with respect to our various problems
and their possible interconnections may be gained by attending briefly
to a few of the most important historical conversations that have re-
volved around faith.

One of these discussions is concerned with the apparent irrele-
vance of faith to action. It is evidently possible for men to believe
—not only to profess belief—in one thing and yet to act in opposition to that belief. In a sociological study of "The Negro Problem"
in America the "American Creed"—significantly so called—was contrasted with American practice; and the dilemma of the nation was
discovered in the conflict between its faith and its action. "The 'American Dilemma,'" writes the author, Gunnar Myrdal, "is the ever-raging
conflict between, on the one hand, the valuations preserved on the
general plane which we shall call the 'American Creed,' where the
American thinks, talks, and acts under the influence of high national
and Christian precepts, and, on the other, the valuations on specific
planes of individual and group living, where personal and local interests; economic, social, and sexual jealousies; considerations of community prestige and conformity; group prejudice against particular
persons or types of people; and all sorts of miscellaneous wants, impulses, and habits dominate his outlook."[4] The problem is not pe-
culiarly American. Continental and colonial charges leveled against
"perfidious Albion" have had their counterpart in English searchings
of conscience as the professed and genuine "beliefs" of the nation were
contrasted with its behavior in the conduct of foreign relations and its
treatment of "lesser breeds without the law." Similar problems have
arisen everywhere when nations or other groups have espoused principles and not been content with the simple aims of surviving and
being powerful. On another level, the hiatus between faith and prac-

4. Gunnar Myrdal, *An American Dilemma: The Negro Problem and Modern
Democracy,* 2 vols. (New York: Harper and Brothers, 1944), 1:xlvii; see especially
the introduction and chapter 1 throughout. [In the original the quoted words are
italicized. (Editor's note.)]

tice appears when one observes how similar may be the actions of men who profess profoundly divergent principles; how dissimilar the actions of those who hold an apparently common faith. It was impossible in Hitler's Germany to predict on the basis of a man's religious, philosophical or political beliefs whether he would resist or succumb to tyranny. The concentration camps of totalitarianisms continue to select on the basis of common action strangely heterogeneous companies of incongruous believers.

The problem of faith and action has been discussed most vehemently and perhaps most acutely in connection with explicitly religious faith. "Faith," wrote Nietzsche in his *Anti-Christ*, "was at all times, for example in Luther, only a cloak, a pretext, a screen behind which the instincts played their play—a shrewd *blindness* about the dominance of *certain* instincts. . . . One always spoke of 'faith' but one acted always from instinct." [5] Similar reproaches against religious faith as at best irrelevant to action, at worst as fraudulent in disguising venality, may be encountered in the writings of skeptics in all centuries. But what is matter for indictment by accusers is the subject of exhortation, confession and soul searching among believers. Christians have been concerned with the problem from their earliest days onward. The Letter of James states it vigorously:

> What does it profit, my brethren, if a man says he has faith but has not works? Can his faith save him? . . . [Faith] by itself, if it has no works, is dead. . . . You believe that God is one; you do well. Even the demons believe—and shudder. . . . [As] the body apart from the spirit is dead, so faith apart from works is dead. (2:14–26)

The question so raised in the Christian community has been endlessly debated by churchmen and others. There seems to be general agreement among them that while there is a faith that is not relevant to action, there is also something in the human mind, also called faith, that is so relevant, and there is some connection between the two kinds of faith. They have been distinguished, following the suggestion of the Letter of James, as dead and living faith. The former does nothing;

5. See Walter A. Kaufmann, *Nietzsche: Philosopher, Psychologist, Anti-Christ* (Princeton: Princeton University Press, 1950), 299–307.

the latter issues in action. Dead faith is belief in propositions, such as that God is one; living faith includes love. So Thomas Aquinas, accepting this terminology, explains that lifeless faith is purely intellectual while living faith is both intellectual and voluntary. In the former the intellect is directed toward its proper end, the First Truth, but in living faith the will also is directed toward its end, the Divine Good. Thomas, however, rejects the idea that lifeless or purely intellectual faith is worthless; it does have preliminary value for those who are perfected to a living faith by the redirection of the will.[6] The distinction is a familiar one which has many analogies in nonreligious experience. It arises in all discussions about the relations of belief in facts to devotion to values, though the facts and values in question seem to be of a most mundane or natural order. When a John Dewey seeks to define a common faith, he does so by distinguishing it not only from belief in supernatural realities but also from all rationalism divorced from emotion or human impulses toward affection, compassion and justice.

> Intelligence, as distinct from the older conception of reason, is inherently involved in action. Moreover, there is no opposition between it and emotion. There is such a thing as passionate intelligence, as ardor in behalf of light shining into the murky places of social existence. . . . One of the few experiments in the attachment of emotion to ends that mankind has not tried is that of devotion, so intense as to be religious, to intelligence as a force in social action.[7]

Even in naturalistic philosophy the problem of dead and living faith and of their relations to each other arises. Bertrand Russell's writings, for instance, abound in reflections on the discontinuity between scientific beliefs and the attitudes, emotions and convictions that inspire men to lead the good life.

Cardinal Newman's contribution to the discussion of this problem directs attention less to the subjective factors involved—intellect, emo-

6. St. Thomas Aquinas, *Summa Theologica*, trans. Fathers of the English Dominican Province, 3 vols. (New York: Benzinger Brothers, 1947), II, part II–II, Q. 4, arts. 1–5.
7. John Dewey, *A Common Faith* (New Haven: Yale University Press, 1934), see 79.

tion and will—than to the objects of inactive and active faith. "[Acts] of notional assent and of Inference do not affect our conduct, [while] acts of Belief, that is, of Real Assent, do (not necessarily, but do) affect it." The object of notional assent is a conceptual proposition; belief, however, is assent to the reality of a thing. In notional assent the intellect is active; in real assent the whole man—feeling, seeing, contemplating, acting—is directed toward the real object. When we assent notionally to the statement that God is one, the words "God" and "one" both refer to ideas; in real assent the word God refers to a reality vividly imagined, felt and loved. Only such real assent, that is, assent to reality, vivifies and empowers a man; notional belief, though it be most logically gained by inference from undoubted premises, is feeble in comparison. "Many a man," says Newman,

> will live and die upon a dogma; no man will be a martyr for a conclusion. A conclusion is but an opinion; it is not a thing which *is,* but which we are *'quite sure about'*; and it has often been observed that we never say we are sure and certain without implying that we doubt. . . . Knowledge of premises and inferences upon them,—this is not to live. . . . Why we are so constituted that faith, not knowledge of argument, is our principle of action, is a question with which I have nothing to do; but I think it is a fact. . . . [No] religion has yet been a religion of physics or of philosophy. It has ever been synonymous with revelation. It has never been a deduction from what we know; it has ever been an assertion of what we are to believe. It has never lived in a conclusion; it has ever been a message, a history, or a vision.[8]

The problem of faith and action, or, as they said, of faith and works, presented itself to the Reformers in a peculiar way. They were less concerned about the faith that did not issue in action than about the

---

8. J. H. Newman, *Grammar of Assent* (Garden City, N.Y.: Doubleday, 1955), 87, 89–92. In his *Primacy of Faith* and elsewhere Richard Kroner defines faith in distinction from the kind of belief to which one may be led by reasoning in terms similar to Newman's. He emphasizes particularly the role of the imagination in faith. See *The Primacy of Faith* (New York: Macmillan, 1943), 139ff., 198ff. [See also Kroner, *The Religious Function of Imagination* (New Haven: Yale University Press, 1941). (Editor's note.)]

belief that by means of activity a man could change his fundamental relations to God and fellowmen. Beginning at this point they also distinguished between two kinds of faith. "Observe," wrote Luther

> there are two ways of believing. In the first place I may have faith *concerning* God. This is the case when I hold to be true what is said concerning God. Such faith is on the same level with the assent I give to statements concerning the Turk, the devil and hell. A faith of this kind should be called knowledge or information rather than faith. In the second place there is faith *in* God. Such faith is mine when I not only hold to be true what is said concerning God, but when I put my trust in him in such a way as to enter into personal relations with him, believing firmly that I shall find him to be and to do as I have been taught. . . . Such faith which ventures everything on what it has heard concerning God, be it life or death, constitutes a Christian man, and it receives everything of God it desires. . . . It is a living faith. . . . The word *in* is well chosen and deserving of due attention. We do not say, I believe God the Father or concerning God the Father, but *in* God the Father, *in* Jesus Christ, and *in* the Holy Spirit.[9]

It is noteworthy that while Luther makes a radical distinction between the faith that is a believing of propositions and the faith that is a trusting, yet he also associates them rather closely.

Calvin, though he distinguishes between the various attitudes that go by the name of faith both in the manner of Thomas and of Luther, seems most concerned to define *saving* faith in opposition to a common or general believing in doctrines. Saving faith is that faith "by which the children of God are distinguished from unbelievers, by which we invoke God as our Father, by which we pass from death to life, and by which Christ, our eternal life and salvation, dwells in us." Whereas prepositions, such as *concerning* and *in,* are important for Luther in his distinction of various kinds of faiths, first-person pronouns—*our, we, us*—are significant for Calvin. What distinguishes living from dead faith is the fact that in the former every statement of doctrine "means *me*" or "*us.*" "The principal hinge on which faith

---

9. *Luther's Catechetical Writings*, trans. J. N. Lenker, 2 vols. (Minneapolis: Luther Press, 1907) 1:203.

turns," he writes "is this—that we must not consider the promises
of mercy, which the Lord offers, as true only to others, and not to
ourselves; but rather make them our own, by embracing them in our
hearts. . . . In short, no man is truly a believer, unless he be firmly
persuaded, that God is a propitious and benevolent Father to him." [10]
Despite this emphasis Calvin remained interested in the teaching of
"sound doctrine" as well as in the personal appropriation of it or of
something corresponding to it. So the relation of two sorts of faith
remains a problem in Calvinism as in Lutheranism.

In his own way Kierkegaard was concerned with the question of
faith and action and made his own distinctions between dead and
living faith. He attacked as vehemently as Nietzsche did the hypocrisy
of a Christendom that professing faith in Jesus Christ acts with stolid
indifference to him. He distinguishes between "objective truth" and
"subjective truth," which is "truth-for-me," in a fashion reminiscent
of John Calvin. He notes the difference between believing historical
statements, such as those which assert truths about the Jesus Christ
of the first century, and the faith that achieves "contemporaneous-
ness with Christ." The difference between these faiths is the difference
between what all Christians believe and what the isolated individual
passionately affirms in his solitariness, or, again, it is the difference
between the kind of believing that makes life easy and the kind that
fills it with suffering.[11] Modern theologians, deeply influenced by Kierkegaard, have taken up these themes. So Rudolf Bultmann has sought
to disjoin existential faith from beliefs about history, nature, and the
ethical life, especially from the mythology of the first century with

10. *Institutes of the Christian Religion*, trans. John Allen, 2 vols., 7th ed., rev.
(Philadelphia: Presbyterian Board of Christian Education, n.d.) I, book III, chapter II, sections xiii and xvi.

11. See especially his *Attack upon Christendom*, *Training in Christianity*, and the
Journals. This last named title is a reference to the early one volume edition of
Kierkegaard's journals, *The Journals of Søren Kierkegaard*, edited and translated
by Alexander Dru (Oxford: Oxford University Press, 1938). A few lines from this
edition exemplify the theme: "And so I say to myself: I choose; that historical fact
[of Jesus Christ] means so much to me that I decide to stake my whole life upon
that if . . . That is called risking; and without risk faith is an impossibility . . . to
believe, to wish to believe, is to change one's life into a trial; daily test is the trial
of faith" (No. 1044). [Editor's note.]

which faith is associated in the New Testament. Faith is a matter of radical obedience in a present moment, and this obedience is not the acceptance of any law, traditionally communicated as the content of the divine will. Neither is it the acceptance, in obedience to church or Scriptures, of any propositions about the cosmos, or even about God. It is rather the acceptance by the free and insecure self of the absolute claim made upon it by the transcendent reality encountered in the gospel. Even so, Bultmann is unable to separate such faith completely from beliefs in the historical actuality of Jesus Christ, as presented in the New Testament.[12]

Even so fragmentary a review of some contentions made in the long discussion about faith and action indicates that men have used the word faith to refer to a complex experience or many-faceted attitude of the human self. It seems to be generally agreed that there is such a thing as assent to propositions and that this is a part of faith; but it is also agreed that such belief does not by itself modify conduct, while there is a faith that radically affects attitudes and behavior. The discussion has not yet produced clear-cut, alternative theories about the nature or the structure of faith, but it has called attention to many elements that enter into the human attitude or set of relations designated by the term. It is as though each participant in the discussion affirmed, "Of course there is such a thing as believing statements; and in religion such a thing as believing statements about God, Christ and man; but there's more to faith than that." However when he defined the *more* each speaker directed attention to a different feature. In the one case the faith that goes beyond belief is voluntary devotion to the good; again it is a kind of perceptual or imaginative immediacy of reality; for a third it is trust in a person; for still others it is the personal appropriation of truth or radical obedience in the presence of the Unconditioned. As in so many other cases, a discussion which began with the reflection that there are two sides to any problem issues

12. Rudolf Bultmann, *New Testament Theology*, trans. Kendrick Grobel, 2 vols. (New York: Charles Scribner's Sons, 1951–55), paragraphs 35 and 54; see also "The Christology of the New Testament" in *Faith and Understanding*, trans. L. P. Smith, vol. 1 (London: SCM Press, 1969), especially 273ff., and Bultmann's article on *pistis* in Gerhard Kittel, *Theological Dictionary of the New Testament*, ed. and trans. G. W. Bromiley, vol. 6 (Grand Rapids, Michigan: Wm. B. Eerdmans, 1968).

in the recognition that this bit of experience or reality is multidimensional. "The other side of faith" is not one side. Faith, if indeed it be a whole of some sort, seems to be something like a cube; one of its sides, the top, appears to be visible from every point of view; other sides present themselves variously to various viewers; while the bottom and the inner sides remain unseen by all.

A SECOND series of conversations or debates concerning faith in which men of all sorts participate and which is important not only for religion but for all other human interests and relations revolves around the question of seeing and believing. Scientists engage in it as they analyze their method of inquiry, asking what roles sense-experience, hypotheses, postulates and a priori principles play in it and how likely it is that present-day scientific beliefs about the physical world will be credible a hundred years hence. Historians participate as they seek to understand events they cannot directly experience and use principles of interpretation that are challenged by those who believe in other principles. The conversation is difficult to follow; it is diffuse and leads into the most abstract regions of the theory of knowledge. Impatient listeners, when they do not understand the language in which it is carried on, are often tempted to say that it is a quarrel about words, or that the statements made are meaningless and merely express emotions. Nevertheless, though the continuing dialogue cannot easily be reduced to a few issues, it is instructive to take note of some of the observations that are recurrently made in its course.

An apparently tough-minded common sense has insisted in all ages that "Seeing is believing" and "What I can't see, I never will believe in!" But it is soon reminded that it disbelieves many things it sees, such as the smallness of the stars compared with the earth, while it believes many statements about the existence and nature of things it does not and cannot see, such as certain historical events to which it constantly refers, or principles like those of human equality and justice, or constructs like those of the atom and the unconscious. At the beginning of the conversation seeing and believing seem to be exclusive of each other; seeing is accompanied by assurance, believing by uncertainty. But as the dialogue proceeds it becomes apparent that there is more than one kind of seeing, more than one sort of believing; that the relations between them are intricate; and that assurance is attached in various measures to each.

For Plato, with all his near and remote disciples, the important distinction is not between seeing and believing but between what is seen in sense-experience and what is "seen" by intellectual vision. The temporal world, the world of sense-experience, can never be the object of knowledge but only of true belief; the eternal and universal, unseen by the physical eye, can be the object not only of true belief but of knowledge, of direct vision. In one sphere, one might say, sight is preliminary to true believing, in the other true believing is preliminary to vision.[13] The Thomists are less skeptical of sense-experience; they contrast faith, as referring to the unseen, with both kinds of sight, the sensual and the intellectual, as well as with opinion. It seemed evident to Thomas that "neither faith nor opinion can be of things seen either by the senses or the intellect," for in faith as in opinion the intellect is not moved to assent by the presence of its "proper object" but rather by an act of choice. In the case of opinion such choice is accompanied by doubt and by the fear that the contrary of what is thought is true; when, however, there is "certainty and no fear of the [contrary], there will be faith."[14]

Modern empiricism, less certain than Plato or Thomas about the possibilities of a knowledge that is completely certain, self-evident and unaccompanied by any act of choice, makes no such radical disjunctions between knowledge and belief. It distinguishes rather between more and less probably true beliefs and confines itself to the temporal world. In its most radical form it excludes not only all possibility of "vision" of what cannot be experienced by the senses but also judges all beliefs about such reality to be meaningless. Less radically it regards beliefs of this kind as highly improbable. In any case in this temporal world, where we perceive nothing that we do not interpret, attend to nothing without expectancy or desire, communicate nothing without the aid of historic languages, our statements about what we

13. A. E. Taylor has written instructively on this subject in his essay, "Knowing and Believing." See his *Philosophical Studies* (London: Macmillan, 1934), 366–98.

14. *Summa Theologica*, II, part II–II, Q. 1, art. 4.

see are at all times statements of belief and our beliefs are attended by greater or less uncertainty. No definite dividing line can be drawn between certain knowledge and uncertain belief. The only line that can be drawn is a curve of probability. At its extreme faith may be defined, as by Bertrand Russell, as "a firm belief in something for which there is no evidence."[15]

Problems of faith and sight have, of course, occupied members of the community of Christian believers ever since the earliest hearers of the gospel asked its preachers to produce some sign from heaven validating its truth, or to show them the Father or the resurrected Christ. The New Testament deals with the question at many levels. One early answer contrasted seeing and believing: "faith," it asserted, "is the assurance of things hoped for, the conviction of things not seen" (Heb. 11:1); or "we walk by faith, not by sight" (2 Cor. 5:7). So faith was defined as essentially a relation to the unseen. Though the emphasis in the Letter to the Hebrews is on the unseen future on which the believer relies, yet what is unseen in present and past is also the object of faith, for, it affirms, "by faith we understand that the world was created by the word of God, so that what is seen was made out of things which do not appear" (11:3). Similarly in the Fourth Gospel Jesus Christ is represented as pronouncing his blessing on "those who have not seen and yet believe" (20:29), and in the First Letter of Peter it is the unseen Jesus Christ who is the object of that genuine faith— "more precious than gold"—by which salvation is obtained. "Without having seen him you love him; though you do not now see him you believe in him" (1:8).

The definition of faith as conviction of the reality of the unseen is accompanied in the pages of the New Testament by another one according to which believing is conviction of the reality of what others have seen. So the author of the Gospel of Luke and of Acts begins his account "of the things that have been accomplished among us" by reference to the eyewitnesses while, more explicitly, the Gospel of John concludes with the statement, "Now Jesus did many other signs in the presence of the disciples, which are not written in this book; but these are written that you may believe that Jesus is the Christ, the

15. Bertrand Russell, *Human Society in Ethics and Politics* (New York: Simon and Schuster, 1955), 203.

Son of God, and that believing you may have life in his name" (20: 30–31). The writer of the First Letter of John seeks to aid Christians to have fellowship with the Father and the Son and one another by proclaiming to them "that which was from the beginning, which we have heard, which we have seen with our eyes, which we have looked upon and touched with our hands, concerning the word of life." This life, says the writer, "was made manifest, and we saw it, and testify to it, and proclaim to you the eternal life which was with the Father and was made manifest to us" (1:1–2). Though faith, according to this approach, is a relation to the unseen yet it refers to what was seen in the past by eyewitnesses and to their testimony. The contrast is not between faith and sight but, in part at least, between unbelief and belief in the testimony of those who have seen or claim to have done so. In this context exhortations to believe though one has not seen are mated with injunctions to bear witness to what one has seen or heard.[16]

There is a third line of thought in the New Testament on the relations of faith and sight: believing is itself a kind of seeing. Only faith can "see" what remains hidden to unbelief. "The righteousness of God has been *manifested* . . . through faith in Jesus Christ for all who believe," writes Paul (Rom. 3:21, 22; emphasis added). It is not faith but unbelief that is blind; "the god of this world has blinded the minds of the unbelievers to keep them from seeing the light of the gospel of the glory of Christ" (2 Cor. 4:4). (See also Rom. 1:18–21 and John 12: 35–44.) Demonstration or revelation and faith accompany each other as darkness or veiledness and unbelief do. Faith is the seeing and knowing of that which "no eye has seen, nor ear heard, nor the heart of man conceived" (1 Cor. 2:9), but which is nevertheless presented in immediacy. This is the central affirmation in the whole teaching about the incarnation. The true light that came into the world remained unknown by the world, but those who received him, "who believed on his name," these "beheld his glory" (John 1:9–14).

Later theology discussed the New Testament problem of faith and sight more in terms of faith and understanding, but it repeated the typical affirmations of the New Testament. The Tertullians and Kierkegaards speak of a faith that believes what cannot be understood

16. See Luke 24:48; John 15:27; Rom. 10:14; 1 Cor. 15:1–19; Jude 3; and many other passages, particularly in Acts.

or seen by the mind's eye, not to speak of the physical senses; exponents of biblical or churchly authority require a faith that accepts the testimony of others who claim to have heard, seen and understood what is beyond the competence of the believer himself; for the Christian mystics faith reaches its culmination in vision, and many another believer, less favored with spiritual experiences, affirms with Thomas that "the light of faith makes us see what we believe," or with Luther and Calvin that by grace of the inner operation of the Holy Spirit faith is an "indubitable hearing" of the Word of God.

As in the case of the discussion about faith and action one may accept these various answers as indicative simply of the vagueness or meaninglessness or purely emotional character of communication employing the word *faith*. Or one may accept them with misplaced piety as representing "the mystery of faith" or "the paradox of faith." However, it is also possible that in these various answers something fairly precise is being indicated about the nature of faith and about that complex of relations in which the believer lives in a company of other believers and in the presence of a reality that, unseen and unheard, is known in the signs only faith experiences and interprets.

WHEN we attend to the debates of philosophers and theologians about faith we are struck by the fact that every participant, no matter how he assails the faith of others, expresses some confidence of his own. And then we further note that confidence is usually professed not in one object only but in several and that often the effort to state this faith moves in a kind of circle from a first object to a second and perhaps a third and back to the first. The common, usually unanalyzed, association of faith with such terms as democracy, the people and education, or nature, experience and reason, in popular statements about the things we can rely on has its counterpart in the more careful analyses of academicians.

An example in philosophy of this expression of a pluralistic and circular faith is offered by A. J. Ayer's radical book, *Language, Truth, and Logic*. Having undertaken to show how meaningless all statements about transcendental reality are and all sentences of a religious or moral sort, he expresses his own confidence in sense-experience and the scientific method. "We rely," he writes, "on our senses to substantiate or confute the judgments which are based on our sensations." This is indeed a faith, an expression of sheer trust in what is not sensibly experienced, since the continuity and unity of sense-experience is not something that is sensed. With this reliance upon sense-experience he associates faith in the scientific method and devotion to life's values. "We are entitled to have faith in our [scientific] procedure," Ayer remarks, "just so long as it does the work which it is designed to do— that is, enables us to predict future experience, and so control our environment"; for "it is plain that on our ability to make successful predictions depends the satisfaction of even our simplest desires, including the desire to survive."[17] Though according to his argument all talk about values is meaningless, and purely expressive of emotion, there is an indication here that Mr. Ayer's justification of faith in science is understood by him as based on something more than an emotional "pro-attitude" toward the objects of his personal desires including his desire to survive. A kind of structure of faith emerges in his confession. He relies on science because he is loyal to human life, not his own merely; and because science is based on sense-experience which he trusts. There are three objects of faith here: sense-experience, science and human values. And faith moves in a kind of circle justifying reliance on each one of these objects by reference to the others.

Pluralism in the effort to state faith is found in all the Christian writings. It may have been a question in the early years whether God or Jesus Christ was the first object of faith, and one of the reasons for the development of Trinitarian doctrine was possibly the need to answer the question about the relation of faith in Jesus Christ to faith in the Creator. At all events it seemed necessary to associate faith in the one with faith in the other and also in the Holy Spirit. But there are other objects of faith in Christianity besides the one God in three persons. From its beginnings Protestantism seems to have been caught up in a movement among various objects of faith, when it affirmed that the gospel of God was to be believed because it was in the Bible and that the Bible was to be believed because it was the Word of that God whom the gospel proclaimed. The movement seems to be most

17. Alfred J. Ayer, *Language, Truth, and Logic* (London: Victor Gollancz, 1938), 27, 48, 139.

circular in Calvin. For him faith essentially "consists in a knowledge of Jesus Christ" since "the apprehension of faith is not confined to our knowing that there is a God, but chiefly consists in our understanding what is his disposition toward us," which is impossible without the faith-relation to Christ. However the knowledge of Christ and so of the divine "disposition toward us" can only be received from the "Word" which is the root and foundation of faith. "Faith has a perpetual relation to the word, and can no more be separated from it, than the rays from the sun." But if we are to believe the "Word," that is, the Scriptures, in which Christ and the paternal favor of God are known, we need first

> a previous persuasion of the Divine veracity; any doubt of which being entertained in the mind, the authority of the word will be dubious and weak, or rather will be of no authority at all. Nor is it sufficient to believe that the veracity of God is incapable of deception or falsehood, unless you also admit, as beyond all doubt, that whatever proceeds from him is sacred and inviolable truth.[18]

So to believe is to be persuaded that God through Jesus Christ is our Father, keeping faith with us and benevolent toward us in every way; but to believe this it is necessary to believe the Scriptures; yet in order to believe the Scriptures one must first believe that God is their author and that this author is what the Scriptures affirm him to be, faithful and benevolent. Does not this make belief in the Scriptures the basic faith of Protestants? Throughout the history of Protestantism this conclusion has been drawn many times both by Protestant theologians and by their critics; and yet this answer is regarded as most unsatisfactory by convinced Protestant believers.

In Roman Catholicism pluralism and circularity seem no less evident although in it the church takes the place of Scriptures. Faith, says Thomas Aquinas, has two objects, a "material" one, that is, the content of a statement, such as the doctrine of the Trinity, and a "formal" one, that whereby the former is known.

> Accordingly if we consider, in faith, the formal aspect of the object, it is nothing else than the First Truth. For the faith of which

18. *Institutes*, I, book III, chapter II, section vi.

we are speaking does not assent to anything except because it is
revealed by God. Hence the mean on which faith is based is the
Divine Truth.

This first truth is

manifested in Holy Writ and the teaching of the Church which
proceeds from the First Truth. Consequently whoever does not
adhere, as to an infallible and divine rule, to the teaching of the
Church, which proceeds from the First Truth manifested in Holy
Writ, has not the habit of faith.[19]

It follows that anyone who believes *what* the church believes but does
not believe it *because* the church teaches it is really without faith.
Thus it seems that Roman Catholicism like Protestantism has several
objects of faith and moves in a circle from one to another. Belief in
the First Truth, that is, "things pertaining to the Godhead," requires
for its foundation belief in the Scriptures, which presupposes belief in
a church which teaches that the Scriptures teach the Truth, which in
turn presupposes belief that the church is governed by that God whom
it proclaims.

Mystics and voluntarists who associate with faith in God reliance
on spiritual experience or on the good will to believe in the reality of
good do not escape such manifoldness and apparent circularity in their
arguments and descriptions of faith, any more than do Protestants and
Roman Catholics. In the contentions between religious groups and between these and rationalists or empiricist unbelievers in religion, each
party points out to the other one how circular and dogmatic and unper-
suasive its statement of faith is. In its own case, however, the apparent
circularity of the argument is not felt as a source of weakness but of
strength. The reliance upon life as able to supply a reason for living to
the living and as powerful enough to maintain itself is strengthened by
the movement of this faith toward the sense-experience of the living
and the scientific method that will enable life to survive. And something like this seems true of the faith that moves from God to Jesus
Christ to Scriptures and church and back again to God.

It may, indeed, be that faith is illogical and that this seeming circu-

19. *Summa Theologica*, II, part II–II, Q. 1, art. 1; Q. 5, art. 3.

larity in the confessions of faith is indicative of its emotional or otherwise unrational character. But it may also be that faith is always in
dynamic movement and that the apparent pluralism and circularity in
it give evidence of a complex pattern or structure. It may be at least as
complex as other operations of the mind are, for instance, knowledge
with its movements from rational principles to sense experience and
back again, from society to individual and back again, from subject to
object.

I N the midst of all these questionings and arguments about faith;
in the controversies of the religious sects and philosophical schools;
among the contentions as defenders of this and that faith attack others
with different beliefs, we become aware of a strange fact. Belief and
disbelief, trust and distrust, fidelity and infidelity toward one another
is present in all those who contend or agree with each other as they
argue about faith. Defensiveness of one's own beliefs and suspicion of
those with other beliefs, distrust of their intellectual ability or honesty
accompany men in all their encounters with each other. Confessions of
loyalty to values of one sort or another and of reliance upon powers,
no less than the implicit and explicit confessions of doubt or confidence in one another can be heard in the midst of all these arguments
and analyses. Belief and trust and fidelity and their opposites are forever present as active attitudes in the very subjects who make them
the objects of their inquiry or disputation. We read the statements of
Thomas Aquinas, Newman, Luther, Calvin, Plato, Bertrand Russell
and John Dewey on the subject of faith with certain predispositions
of trust or distrust. Complete disinterestedness may be possible in our
encounter with things or even thoughts. But as we deal with thinking men we raise the questions: Can they be trusted? Where are they
trying to lead me? What are they defending? This page is being read
with some trust or distrust of the writer as a person or as representing
a class; it is being written also with overtones of trust and distrust in
readers of various classes, of fidelity and infidelity to a cause.
    Questions *about* faith, about its relations to action, to sight and
understanding, about its objects and circular movements are important
to us only because we have previously been required to answer the
questions *of* faith. These have been put to us in direct encounter with
all the objects of our trust and distrust, belief and disbelief, loyalty and

infidelity. The primary situation in which faith appears as a problem is of the sort in which Descartes found himself as he looked upon the "very proud and magnificent palaces" erected by ancient moralists and discovered he distrusted them as being "built on nothing but sand and mud." Or, on the positive side, it is the situation in which he answers the question about what he can believe by affirming his own existence on the basis of confrontation with himself as thinking being.[20] Faith appears in problematic form, as faith in question, in all the Hamlet-like discoveries we make of the contradiction between the appearance in which we believed and the reality that now seems to manifest itself. When "this goodly frame, the earth," becomes a "sterile promontory"; when the heavens, "this majestical roof fretted with golden fire," turns into a "foul and pestilent congregation of vapours"[21]; when the corruption of the trusted king and of the apparently loyal wife and mother are brought to light; or when, in less existential forms, the possible deceptiveness of the familiar world of color, warmth and fragrance is brought home to our minds; then the belief and disbelief, the trust and distrust, the fidelity and treachery in existence come into view. Then the direct question of faith is put to us.

We hear it raised in encounters of another sort, when familiar disbelief is challenged. Then it may be the sort of question Jesus raised for his disciples: "Why are you so fearful, O you of little faith?" or put to Mary: "I am the resurrection and the life. . . . Do you believe this?" (Matt. 8:26; John 11:25, 26).[22]

---

20. Rene Descartés, "Discourse on the Method for Rightly Conducting One's Reason and for Seeking Truth in the Sciences"; the references are to part 1 and part 4. Which edition of Descartés the author used is not definitely ascertainable; however, the reader may consult the translation by Donald A. Cress in *Discourse on Method and Meditations on First Philosophy* (Indianapolis: Hackett, 1980), 4, 17. [Editor's note.]

21. The phrases are from *Hamlet* (II, ii). [Editor's note.]

22. It seems that in the draft stage of writing the author quoted the Bible from memory and drew upon several translations, including Luther's translation into the German, the Authorized (King James) Version and the Revised Standard Version (RSV). Generally, but not always, I have brought punctuation and orthography into conformity with the RSV. Here in the case of Matt. 8:26 I have let "fearful" stand, which is the word the Authorized Version uses, although the RSV reads "afraid." [Editor's note.]

We become aware of these primary questions of faith usually in those times when our confidence in the hitherto trusted is shaken or when we are moved to rely on the previously untried; but they are being constantly addressed to us in all our daily encounters with our companions and our world. They accompany like an undertone all the transactions and communications between men and all their dialogues of perception and conception with common objects. We are forever being asked and asking: Do you believe me? Do you trust me? Are you trustworthy and believable? Are you faithful to me and to our common cause?

2

THE METHOD OF REFLECTION

Faith seeks understanding in a double way. It seeks to understand what it believes but also how it believes. As man the knower seeks clarity about his knowing activities as well as about known realities, as man the valuer finds himself impelled to inquire into his choosing no less than into the nature of chosen and rejected values, so believing man wants to know how he believes as well as what he believes. Why man is obliged or compelled to pursue such insight he may not know this side of its achievement. He recognizes that he needs such insight because without critical awareness of subjective activity he cannot exercise critical discrimination among its objects.

In the endeavor to gain this knowledge no other method seems to be available to us than that of reflection. Insight into the self and its activities, as these are directed toward their objects, does not come with external observation. One cannot point to subjective activities such as perceiving, conceiving, valuing, or believing and say "Lo, here!" or "Lo, there!" It is only by looking within ourselves and catching as it were the reflections of ourselves in act that we are able to achieve some degree of critical self-awareness.

So the reflective method is subjective, in the sense that the reflecting self takes as its object one of its activities as a subject. It does not need therefore to fall into the error of a subjectivism that abstracts subjective activity from its objects. Though in reflection one does not attend primarily to these objects, one does not need to lose sight of them, any more than when one attends to objects one needs . . . to lose sight of the subjective activities directed toward them. In reflection on my perceiving I may indeed so overrate the importance of my subjective activity in comparison with the action on me of the perceived objects as to be led into asserting the complete dependence of object on subject. But it need not be so; the method of reflection does not necessarily lead to this conclusion; it does not presuppose the primacy of the subjective. Though we undertake . . . to begin our inquiry by attending to the activity of believing in its relatedness to the believ*ed* or believed *in,* we do not assume that the method of reflection begins at the beginning of reality. How faith is related to its object is one of the questions that reflection seeks to answer.

When we use the reflective method we attend primarily to ourselves; we are concerned with self-knowledge. If we do not begin with external observation of other men who say they are believing, or valuing, or knowing, neither do we begin with impersonal assertions and ideas. We do not make statements about faith the primary object of our inquiry, asking about their truth or falsity, their precision or imprecision, their tautological or synthetic character, their meaning or meaninglessness. Neither do we examine ideas of faith, our own ideas, those of others, or the ideas of reason as such, seeking to define the true idea. It is to ourselves in the activities we call believing and having faith that we attend, seeking to make significant statements about ourselves as believers and endeavoring to achieve adequate ideas.

However, the reflective method is not solipsistic. We can carry on our effort to understand ourselves only in the company of other selves whom we are trying to understand and who are trying to understand themselves and us. The reflective method is always interpersonal, dependent on communication, seeking verification, correction, guidance from the reflections of others as these are mediated through statements about faith and definitions of the idea of faith. We do not even seem to know ourselves as selves in isolation but only in interpersonal society, in which we communicate with each other about common objects, whether these be the objects of perception or of reflection. The long history of the fruitful discussions that have been carried on in the theory of knowledge, in ethics and reflective theology indicate that the method of reflection is not less social and interpersonal in character than is the method of external observation. Though it begins its inquiry by attending to the self it does not assume that the self is the beginning of its own activities, including this activity of reflection.

Reflection on faith, like every other reflective inquiry, must begin

. . . right in the middle of things. It cannot "begin at the beginning" of the dialogue between subject and object or of the dialogue between self and other selves. Nor can it begin at some point in the self outside of the activity that is the object of reflection. It must perforce accept not only the actuality of its object but of the presence in the reflecting self of the very activity that is being objectified. When we ask ourselves how it is that we know anything, we are exercising that same activity of knowing which we are trying to know. When we examine our valuing, choosing, our self-legislating and our obeying or disobeying, we are at the same time valuing, legislating and obeying or disobeying, since in the inquiry itself we must distinguish between the important and unimportant, must be subject to discipline and under obligation; we are obliged, at the very least, to be honest with ourselves. So also when we reflect on believing, with all the other activities connected with it, we do so as those who must accept the fact that we are believing (or doubting) subjects in the very presence of our own believing. We ask ourselves in the very act of trying to understand our believing whether we can trust our observations, whether we are adequately disinterested, whether others who offer us their definitions and reflections on our believing and theirs are trustworthy, or have some special axe to grind. Believing is present to us when we seek to know believing. Of course, these various activities cannot be abstracted from each other; in reflection the whole self is present in all of its activity. When it seeks to know its knowing it also values and believes; when it values its valuing it does so as a discriminating, believing-doubting self; it believes and doubts its knowing and valuing.

Because the method of reflection seems to invite an infinite regress into subjectivism by a self that pursues images of itself, reflected, as it were, in opposing mirrors; because it is subject to many errors and self-deceptions; because it seems far removed from the practical concerns and problems of men in personal, living encounter with physical, ideal, moral and divine challenges issuing from an objective world; therefore it is often brushed aside by those who believe that there are more direct ways to knowledge, assurance and right action. The impatience of psychologists with the "introspective" method, the positivistic turn in philosophy from self-knowledge to the knowledge of objects—even when no other object than language is available—are matched in theology by the rejection of the reflective method, especially as this was practiced by Schleiermacher and his successors. Instead of inquiring into faith by means of a *Glaubenslehre*,[1] it seems more faithful to make the Scriptures the object of inquiry and to ask with biblical theology, "What do the men of the Bible believe?" To others it seems more in keeping with the faith by which they live to ask, "What does the church believe?" and so to set forth a dogmatic theology. Or again, when it is recognized that faith in God cannot be based on anything except itself, then it seems more faithful to try to lead men by means of indirect communication or by direct proclamation to that immediate encounter with the God of faith in which alone faith comes into being. Hence theology, it appears, must be either "existential" or "kerygmatic." Each of these methods serves an important purpose, yet none of them can do the particular work which reflective theology undertakes to do, and this work is as necessary as self-examination and self-knowledge are in any other sphere of the life of the self. In that life there are the existential faith-questions addressed to the self by the realities it faces in encounters of trust and distrust, belief and unbelief; there are confessional faith-questions addressed to it by companions who ask for reports of these encounters; but there are also reflective faith-questions in which we ask ourselves, in our societies, about what we have done and do in these encounters and confessions. And these questions of the third order need to be answered if our answers to existential and confessional questions are to be given with some assurance. When we remember all the illusions and errors, all the distrusts and uncertainties, all the dishonesties and evasions, all the treasons and breaches of faith as well as all the positive gifts that mark the history of this human activity of believing, confessing and keeping faith we can no more avoid the task of self-criticism and clarification in this sphere than we can avoid similar reflective labor in dealing with a

---

1. *Glaubenslehre* is here a reference to Friedrich Schleiermacher's *The Christian Faith*. In German the title of this work is *Der Christliche Glaube*. But Schleiermacher and others commonly refer to it as his *Glaubenslehre*, literally, doctrine of faith. Here HRN is referring to the specific idea of dogmatic theology that Schleiermacher adopted, namely, the view that dogmatic propositions set forth Christian religious affections. The critics to whom HRN refers objected that Schleiermacher fell into subjectivism. [Editor's note.]

knowledge that is subject to many errors and a morality that is full of desires for deceptive good and of obedience to perverted imperatives.

W H E N we try to deal reflectively with the faith that believes in God, in men, in causes, in church, in Scriptures, we make our way among hazards. Some of them are indicated to us by the warnings of objectors to the method itself; others by the misfortunes of previous inquirers who have followed this way. It must be taken for granted that we shall encounter and in part succumb to these as well as to other perils. But there are no safe roads in theological inquiry, if, indeed, there are sure paths in any human search for knowledge. The venture must be made. Yet it will be well if we remind ourselves of some of these dangers that we must try to avoid.

One set of perils is encountered when we are tempted to try to transcend the subject-object situation of the self and to seek a kind of knowledge impossible for us, a knowledge without duality. The situation of the dialogue, in which there is no self without an other, no subject without an object and vice versa, is the given situation in which all our knowing takes place. No data are given to us without a sensing, no ideas without a conceiving, no values without a desiring, no world without a knowing, no selves and no gods without a believing. On the other hand none of these activities is present in the self without the objects toward which they are directed. Impatient with this "egocentric predicament" we often seek a knowledge of things as they are in themselves and of ourselves as we are in ourselves. Thus we try to transcend the subject-object situation; but it accompanies us in the very effort we make to get outside it and so we fall either into an inconsistent, self-contradictory objectivism or into an equally inconsistent subjectivism.

When we center our attention on the subjective activity of faith we may assume that it is self-originated, that it is the creator of its objects and that it is deceptive so far as it posits their independent existence. The gods of faith, we are inclined to say then, are wish-beings; out of our great longing for something or someone on whom to rely for meaning we create our deities; the will to believe is the author of the creed. Faith in the Father in heaven is the great illusion which can be explained away by anyone who has accurate knowledge of the psychology of believing subjects. This subjectivism with respect to faith can be supported by reference to the deceptions to which believing men fall prey, to the idols they have fashioned in their own image or in the images of familiar love and trust. Yet it is impossible by means of subjectivism to escape from the dialectical subject-object situation in which we believe someone or something. The subjectivist asserts in act what he denies in words. When he asserts that faith creates the gods he implies at the same time that he is able to be sure of this because he is in relation to an object that can be depended upon as independent of his own existence and as powerful apart from his confidence in it. So the Feuerbachs challenge faith in the supernatural gods and regard these as wish-beings, or as the self-projected images of believing men, while asserting at the same time their confidence in the human race as a reality that creates and supports enduring values. They do not assert confidence in their own subjective selves but in mankind, independent in existence and in worth of the selves that trust and believe in it.[2] So also the so-called rationalist or "scientific" attacks on religious believing, as entirely subjective and on its objects as projections, assert or imply confessions of confidence in something that is objective, such as reason or the scientific method or some other actuality or activity distinct from and independent of that activity of confidence which is directed toward it. In every attack on another man's faith as a subjective projecting of illusory gods, there is implicit an activity of believing in a reality or power that is not subjective. That there is much illusion, much projection, in the activity of believing is undeniable; but criticism and discrimination are possible in this realm only as one subject-object relation is compared with another, not as the whole activity of believing is dismissed as objectless.

On the other hand the effort may be made to transcend the subject-object situation by asserting the sole reality of the object. But when the endless dialogue is so reduced to a monologue on the part of the object

2. Ludwig Feuerbach, after arguing "The True or Anthropological Essence of Religion," states that he has demonstrated that "God" is but the name for human nature alienated from itself and that "Man" is the actual object of human devotion. Accordingly Feuerbach concludes part 1 of *The Essence of Christianity* with the proposition, "The beginning, middle, and end of Religion is MAN." This actual object of religion, "Man," has all the positive attributes of "God." See Ludwig Feuerbach, *The Essence of Christianity*, trans. Marian Evans (New York: Calvin Blanchard, 1855). [Editor's note.]

and it is maintained that there is a believing or a knowing that depends wholly on the object, then the protagonist of this position abandons it in the very act of seeking to communicate it. For in the act of communication he presupposes the presence of the sort of subjective activity that he is denying in those companions whose knowledge or faith he is seeking to correct or enlighten; he must also acknowledge that his own speech at least is something else than an echo or reflection of the object to which he refers. He cannot avoid confessing that he is a subject distinctly different from the object and is directing attention, not simply to the object, but to himself as testifying about that object. I cannot maintain that the blueness of the sky is "really" there in the sky and not in my sensation without appealing to my seeing, to the seeing of my companions and without asserting that it is my subjective conviction that the blueness is objective. The presence of the subject and the acceptance of the dialogue between subject and object cannot be evaded in discussions about faith any more than in discussions about sensation, conception and valuation. Karl Barth, in his reaction against all subjectivist tendencies in theology, insists that God is "the source of all knowledge of Himself" and that "he wills to be known through no one except through Himself." "Faith knowledge," he maintains, ". . . is a type of knowledge which is unconditionally bound to its object."[3] In saying so much, however, he is at least presupposing that such statements and convictions about faith and God are not God's statements but Karl Barth's. He is calling attention to his own presence as a knowing and believing subject as well as to the object of knowing and believing; he is also acknowledging the presence of other believing subjects, whom he is addressing, who may not only be mistaken about their faith but in their faith. Moreover such objectivism recognizes the dialectical character of the situation in which faith and revelation, the knowledge of God and God, are present by including in its theory of objective revelation the teaching about the Holy Spirit with his internal testimony to the objective reality.[4] The objectivist can

3. Karl Barth, *The Knowledge of God and the Service of God According to the Teaching of the Reformation*, trans. J. L. M. Haire and Ian Henderson (London: Hodder and Stoughton, 1938), 19, 20, 26.
4. Karl Barth, *Church Dogmatics* (New York: Charles Scribner's Sons, 1956), vol. 1, part 2, "The Holy Spirit the Subjective Possibility of Revelation," 242ff.

no more begin outside the subject-object dialogue than can the subjectivist. He can only believe, know, think, criticize, discriminate and confess in the midst of it. He can only compare one subject-object relation with another, or the objects that are the counterpart of one kind of subjective activity with those that accompany another kind, or the subjective activities that are directed to certain objects with those that are directed toward others.

The acceptance of the subject-object duality as the unavoidable situation in which we must carry on all our thinking and which we cannot transcend does not imply the acceptance of a specific theory of knowledge save insofar as the rejection of self-contradictory subjectivism and self-contradictory objectivism implies the acceptance of a critical theory. The way of reflection is not mapped and defined when the perils on the right and the left are discerned; it may turn out to be a narrow strait between a Scylla and a Charybdis; but it may also be a broad pass that allows thoroughfare from various approaches. As we undertake to reflect on faith and its structure, we need only accept the fact that we are engaged in a constant dialogue between I and Thou or It. We cannot understand our believing and unbelieving, our trusting and distrusting, our keeping faith and our faithlessness, our relations of faith to men and the gods or God, by attempting to get outside of the dialogical situation in which our breaches of faith as well as our errors of understanding occur. We can only continue the dialogue and in the midst of it try to understand ourselves as well as the other, the object. . . .

3

BELIEVING AND KNOWING

When we seek guidance for our reflective inquiry into faith from those who have explored this matter before, we soon realize that they direct attention to two different elements in our personal activity or attitude that are both called *believing*. One group examines the feelings of certainty or uncertainty that accompany our action when we hold something to be true; the other is concerned with the activity of trusting in someone or something. In the one case belief is defined as "conviction of the truth or reality of a thing based on grounds insufficient for positive knowledge"; in the other as "a state or habit of mind in which trust is placed in some person or thing." Doubtless we find both of these elements present in our experience—feelings of conviction and actions of trust; doubtless they are often closely associated; hence we need not engage in a fruitless discussion about the "real" meaning of the word *belief* but only determine which of them will best repay further examination.

Kant, developing a long tradition in philosophy, is one of those who describe belief in terms of the sense of certainty attaching to conviction of truth. "The holding of a thing to be true," writes Kant

> has the following degrees [or stages, *Stufen*]: *opining, believing,* and *knowing. Opining* is such holding of a judgment as is consciously insufficient, not only objectively, but also subjectively. If our holding of the judgment be only subjectively sufficient, and is at the same time taken as being objectively insufficient, we have what is termed *believing.* Lastly, when the holding of a thing to be true is sufficient both subjectively and objectively, it is *knowledge.*[1]

1. Immanuel Kant, *Critique of Pure Reason*, trans. Norman Kemp Smith (London: Macmillan, 1950), 646.

A. E. Taylor agrees in part, assigning to belief a degree of assurance that opinion lacks though its distinction from knowledge is not to be described in psychological terms. "There is a state of mind," he believes (or opines or knows) "that is neither wavering and uncertain opinion, nor yet knowledge (even on the view . . . that absolutely assured conviction is knowledge, when that of which we feel the assurance is true), and for this state of mind I can find no other name in our language than belief."[2] Now it does seem true that we experience various degrees of the feeling of conviction, but whether these can be at all sharply separated from each other into stages, names assigned to the stages and each of them associated with specifically defined grounds seems highly questionable. Clear distinction between the subjective and objective is always difficult; but even if it could be made, there are degrees of subjective and of objective adequacy. Moreover the comparison of the degree of conviction that one subject feels with that of another is difficult if not impossible. Feelings of assurance or conviction are doubtless present in us as we hold statements to be true, but the inquiry into the nature or degrees or grounds of these feelings seems likely to involve us in solipsistic inquiries and in the making of arbitrary definitions that do not lead beyond themselves.

That activity called believing which is a trusting in another person offers a more fruitful prospect for inquiry. It is involved in much of that holding for true to which Kant directs attention. A. E. Taylor, having distinguished belief from opinion psychologically, as being certain where the latter is wavering, distinguishes it from knowledge not by lack of assurance but by the indirectness of its relation to an object about which it has a conviction. Says he, "The whole of what can properly be called 'theory of knowledge' is contained in an answer to the question, 'does knowing differ from opining and believing?' And the true answer to this question can be given in three words, 'By being vision.'"[3] True knowing, whether in perception or by "the mind's eye" is "direct and immediate apprehension of truth." Belief, then, like opinion is an indirect relation to the object about which we hold something to be true. In what way then is it indirect? In many if

2. A. E. Taylor, "Knowing and Believing," *Philosophical Studies*, 374.
3. A. E. Taylor, "Knowing and Believing," *Philosophical Studies*, 398, 386.

not in most cases when we hold something to be true without having a direct relation to the truth or its object, we have a relationship to it via a person we trust. A logician, describing belief in the sense of Kant as a kind of conviction about truth, distinguishes five ways in which we attain it. First, we may believe something "because we have always believed it"; second, we may believe on authority, that is, because someone whom we respect, either because of his office or because he is an expert in the subject matter concerned, asserts it to be true; in the third place, "we may attain belief by the way of self-evidence, that is, because the truth seems obvious"; fourth, we may believe by way of persuasion, under the influence of rhetoric or advertising; and, finally, we may believe by way of conviction through reasoning.[4] In the last of these cases the indirectness of our relation to the object about which we hold something to be true is the indirectness of inference; in the third, the way of self-evidence, we may be dealing with what Taylor would call knowledge; but in the other three instances the way to belief is through trusted persons *whom we believe*. What we have always believed is what we have been taught in childhood by respected adults and have not been led to doubt by other companions or by personal experience; it is what our community believes without discussion or dissension; it is often the set of convictions that constitute the climate of opinion which even bitter intellectual antagonists share. What we believe on the authority of officials or of experts and what we believe as a result of persuasion we hold also as the result of the mediation of other persons, though there are differences between the trust we repose in authority or the expert on the one hand, the propagandist on the other. Whether or not the kind of feeling of certainty that our first group of inquirers call belief is always indirect in this sense of being related to its object through the mediation of a trusted other person, in any case there is a close connection between much of our "holding for true" and our trusting. It is to our believing in this sense as our holding for true on the ground of trust in another that we can hopefully direct our inquiry, leaving aside the question of the degree of conviction-feeling that accompanies it.

4. See L. S. Stebbing, *A Modern Introduction to Logic* (London: Methuen, 1930), 466ff.

Believing in this sense seems to constitute by far the major part of our intellectual furniture and of the basis of our daily actions. Our understanding of nature to which we like to give the honorific title of science or knowledge is for the greater part of educated, as of uneducated, men largely a matter of belief. Very few know with anything like directness of vision the truths they hold about the solar system and the stars, about the elements and their atomic weights, about the structure of the atoms and their nuclei, about bacteria and viruses, or even about the physiological and psychological processes of their own bodies and minds. We hold these truths on authority—on the authority of the community of scientists, on the authority of our doctors, of our teachers, of the writers of monographs and encyclopedias. Our understanding of history is even more evidently an affair of believing statements about events to which we have little direct relationship, and of which we have little knowledge in the sense of direct experience. In historical inquiry much of our effort is spent in trying to discover how trustworthy our various mediators of knowledge are; here we endeavor to know in order that we may believe. Historical science is necessarily directed for the most part to criticism of documents, to inquiry into trustworthiness.

When we analyze the situation in which we believe and know, or, better, have direct and indirect relations to objects about which we hold something to be true, with more or less feeling of assurance, we are made aware of something that logicians and epistemologists, and many reflective religious thinkers also, strangely ignore—the social nature of our knowing and believing. Trusting, holding for true, and even knowing (the direct relation) have their place not in that isolated situation in which a subject confronts an object but in a social situation in which a self in the company of other selves deals with a *common* object. In the actual human situation a believing enters into all our knowing and a knowing into all our believing. Believing and knowing, being certain and uncertain, trusting and having vision of true relations, these are events that occur only in interpersonal society. There are no mind-object or I-It relations that can be intelligibly abstracted from mind-mind and I-Thou relations, nor do there seem to be any interpersonal or inter-mental relations that can be understood without reference to common objects. This much neglected social character of knowing and believing requires further exploration.

WHEN we reflect on our direct "vision," our knowing of objects, we often ignore the fact that a coknower is always present to us in this situation of direct encounter. When I try to analyze what I am doing in knowing this paper, these letters, this white and black immediately before me and what I mean when I assert, apparently to myself, "I know this paper; I perceive these letters; I know that this paper is white and not black," I may easily forget with many another inquirer that all this perceiving and knowing and making of statements is carried on in society. I seem to myself to be alone with my objects and the apprehension of them seems direct, without any mediation. Yet I recall that this whole train of reflections on my knowing has been initiated by the questions of companions and in my effort to formulate them I cannot but have in mind the companion knowers for whom I am formulating them as I state them to myself. Would there be any reflection, would there be anything but brute immediacy, without even the knowledge that it is immediacy, had there not been these coknowers and coinquirers into knowledge in my past and were there not coknowers in my future whose questions and reflections I anticipate?

As the process of reflection is social, so the content of the reflections is social also. So far as it is stated in words this is evident, for the words are those of my society and I try to understand myself in my situation by means of words that have been spoken and written by others in similar situations. At the same time I endeavor to make others understand my reflections by using words that will direct them to situations like my present one. The words refer to ideas and the ideas to specific objects, named "paper," "letters," "black," and so forth. Words and concepts all have a double reference: on the one hand they mean objects, they direct attention to objects; on the other hand they are directed to persons, as words and concepts also in the minds of my fellow-knowers by means of which they will be directed toward the same objects. All my certainties and doubts in this situation are also social. The assurance that I have that this is paper which I see is an assurance that my fellow-knowers confronting this object will not only use the same word for it but, more importantly, will define it in the same way, by reference to origin and purpose as well as various qualities. My doubts are social doubts as I question whether these reflections will be corroborated by others who reflect on their perceptions of similar objects, and on the variety of words used to designate what I call "paper"; but even more my doubts are social doubts as I reflect on the variety of definitions in different cultures of this object that to me and my coknowers is writing paper but would be directly known as a different object by members of an illiterate society. My knowledge, then, seems to be through and through a social knowledge, even in its immediacy. It is not social in the sense that society is its object, but in the sense that it participates in the society's knowledge of objects; it is my knowledge as that of a self who has companion knowers and who without such companions knows nothing, for what is true of my perceptions of objects seems even more true of those direct "visions" of true relations that are apprehended by "the mind's eye."

In this situation a trusting of other persons and a believing of their statements about objects that we also know directly enters into all our objective knowledge. Knowing begins with such social believing as its accompaniment, is continued in constant association with social believing and gains its assurance in the midst of social believing. It begins with believing or in association with believing as when in childhood we take on trust the statements of our companions about objects to which we either have no direct relations or which we cannot sort out of the confusion of sensation without the aid of social categories. We memorize the multiplication table as we memorize the Ten Commandments. We have no direct relation at the time to things in large numbers or to the large numbers in things which that table represents. But the complete assurance of parents and teachers that $12 \times 12 = 144$ is communicated to us and we believe it with certainty. If knowledge means direct vision we do not have knowledge of these highly abstract objects in their relations, or of concrete things in these complex relations. But by believing we are put in the way of gaining direct knowledge as we encounter things in the gross, and numbers in perceived objects. What is true in this instance seems to be true in all others. All the words we use and the concepts associated with the words indicate the acceptance on trust of the statements of our fellow-knowers. Language and knowledge are inseparably interwoven and language is received in trust and belief. "The language of our mother tongue," as a philosophically minded linguist points out,

> determines not only the way we build sentences but also the way
> we view nature and break up the kaleidoscope of experience into

objects and entities about which to make sentences. We cut up and organize the spread and flow of events as we do largely because, through our mother tongue, we are parties to an agreement to do so, not because nature itself is segmented in exactly that way. . . . English terms, like "sky," "hill," "swamp," persuade us to regard some elusive aspect of nature's endless variety as a distinct *thing*, almost like a table or a chair. Thus English and similar tongues lead us to think of the universe as a collection of rather distinct objects and events corresponding to words. Indeed, this is the implicit picture of classical physics or astronomy—that the universe is essentially a collection of detached objects of different sizes.

We usually remain unaware of the effect of language on our knowledge, whether of natural or other events, and so of the partial dependence of direct knowledge on society, and so of our personal knowledge on our believing our companions, until our beliefs are challenged by another set of beliefs. We blithely assert that a thing is what it is and not something else until we discover that there are other knowers and believers who organize the flowing events of experience in other patterns than we do, though they are not less directly related to the flow than we are. There are some languages, such as Hopi, the linguist points out "in which the means of expression are not as separate as in English, but flow together in plastic, synthetic creations. Hence such languages . . . point toward possible new types of logic and possible new cosmical pictures."[5] How much knowledge of nature depends on language and the logic inherent in language the example of mathematics also indicates. Mathematics with its symbols and signs is a very precise language which enables us not only to communicate about but also to know some highly precise features in our experience. It is a language that is largely acquired through believing—the social language of a community. But it is quite impossible to know with the aid of that language what can be known with the aid of the language of dramatists and poets, a language that must also be acquired through believing trusted fellowmen. The world known through the mediation

5. Bejamin Lee Whorf, "Languages and Logic," *Technology Review* 43, no. 6 (April 1941). Reprinted in Laura Thompson, *Culture in Crisis: Study of the Hopi Indians* (New York: Harper and Brothers, 1950), 153f.

of the one language is not more directly encountered than the world known through the other; the precise objects and precise relations of which we have "vision" are not more objective than the boundless passions, aspirations and emotions of men that the other set of symbols and concepts enables us to identify. Knowing and believing, subject and fellow-subject, are present in each set of subjective encounters with objective realities.

We are not justified in drawing a radically skeptical conclusion from this recognition of the dependence of our knowing on our social language and our trusting of our fellowmen with their language-communicated logic and worldviews. It does not follow that because English-speaking people encounter hills and valleys where Hopi see ground in motion, "there are no hills and vales but speaking makes them so." To realize that our direct encounters with undulations of the ground are all modified by our acceptance of the explicit and implicit definings of things by our society, neither means that our companions in the society did not encounter these movements nor that they are not there. Neither does it mean that we cannot correct indefinitely in the course of continuing dialogues with nature and each other the ideas, concepts, relations we have taken on trust. It does mean that an element of believing, of acceptance of the reports of our companions, of the tradition of our society about encounters with nature, enters into all our knowing at the very beginning. When I say: "I know that this is a hill, or paper or a book," I am giving evidence not only of my direct knowledge but of my believing. Of course, this "believing" as trusting of our companions has various degrees of assurance-feeling attached to it.

Our knowing as direct encounter not only begins with believing in this sense but continues to the accompaniment of believing. The great cooperative work of natural and historical scientists is a grand illustration of the common daily process in which we are all involved as we increase our knowledge of ourselves, our political and economic and religious situation, our natural environment, and so forth. We believe and disbelieve each other as communication flows back and forth, in newspapers, journals, conversations, meetings, the reports of fellow-knowers in fields remote from our own, the publication of historical documents. We believe where predecessors disbelieved and disbelieve where they believed. All these knowers, in trusting or distrusting companionships with fellow-knowers, continue their encounters with common objects.

Our direct knowledge attains certainty only in this social setting where it is verified by the experiences and the reports of fellow-knowers. Verification requires not only that the same subject shall find the same consequences in an experiment or in an encounter with the same objective order in repeated instances, but that other subjects find similar or identical results in similar encounters and that *these other subjects be trustworthy*. There are doubtless times when a knower finds skepticism all around him and yet maintains the truth of his own statements, but this purely subjective certainty is never a sufficient criterion of truth. The knower himself appeals to time, to future verification. His society will not accept, will not believe his statements—at least not in the long run—until they are supported by the statements of others whom it trusts. And on the whole it judges rightly; for every Galileo who must wait for verification, there are doubtless hundreds of visionaries and mountebanks whose reports of their encounters and direct relations to objective realities are untrustworthy. In every case believing, as trust in social companions or cosubjects, and knowing, as direct encounter and distinct apprehension of form and relations in the objective order, go together.

The nature of the illustrations which we have used itself illustrates the meaning of the situation. The contemporary age is an age of faith, that is, of trust in science, that is, in the scientists. Only a small fraction of the people have much direct knowledge of the objective order with which the natural scientists are concerned. But they believe the scientists and even insofar as they enter into direct relations with the objective order, natural events of which scientists write, they begin and continue their knowing to the accompaniment of believing the scientists. Because of the prevalence of this believing of social companions in our encounter with nature the illustrations seem apt. But the situation is not fundamentally different when we deal with our human encounters with nonnatural realities, be they called ideal, supernatural or by some other name. The knowledge of those realities with which reason deals in abstraction from perception, most evidently present in mathematics, the difficult knowledge of such qualities as we encounter in painting and music, the even more difficult knowledge of good and evil, above all the most difficult knowledge of the Transcendent, all take place in this social context of believing companions whom we trust. Indeed, to those who are not aware of the directness of their relations to that objective order to which beliefs in these areas refer it will appear that there is *only* belief here and no knowledge at all, only indirect relation through trustworthy or untrustworthy companions. But that is another story to which as to the subject of trustworthiness we must return later on.

As there is a believing of other persons present in all our knowing of the objective order so there is a knowing in all our believing. It is knowing in the sense of being a direct relation, not a believing in the sense of being a knowledge about, gained from an authority or a companion. To be sure, if by knowing we mean analytical understanding of that which we encounter directly, then indeed, this is not knowing. But if we mean by knowing directness of apprehension or "vision" it is a knowing. In order that a distinction may be made, we give to the knowledge present in believing the name *acknowledgment*. What is so acknowledged in our believing is the person.

The acknowledgment of personality or selfhood which is present in believing is first of all the recognition of another knower. When I believe the scientist, as he makes statements about the structure of the atom, I acknowledge the presence of a perceiver and thinker, of a knower who is not my object but who as subject has a relation to an object. The acknowledgment of other knowers is not objective knowledge. Another man as the direct object of my perceiving and conceiving is a body, a form, an activity, or complex of activities, but there is no perception of him as a perceiving being nor is the relation of myself to him that of thinker to concept. I do not conceive the idea of a knower. Yet in the presence of a common object, which may be present to both of us in perception or present to one of us only in imagination while it is present to the other in perception or memory, I acknowledge him as a perceiver and a knower in my believing or disbelieving him; even in disbelieving I acknowledge a subject though I question his communication about the common object. Since all knowing involves this triadic relation of at least two subjects and an object all knowing involves such an acknowledgment of other knowers. Such acknowledgment of others is an inescapable fact. Without it I have no knowledge of anything.

Yet the acknowledgment of the person which takes place in all believing and disbelieving is not only the recognition of an other as subject-knower. Believing the statement of another is an act of trusting a self, of acknowledging the presence of a being who not only knows and as such can be in error, but of one who is bound by promises and as such can betray me, can tell a lie, or can speak truth, can keep faith with me. When we believe a person we acknowledge that there is present to us a moral self, that is, one who is obligated to a cause, a law, and to us, who has bound himself to us by explicit or implicit promises not to deceive us but to be faithful in telling us the truth about what he knows. The truth is not simply a relation between his perception-conception and the object perceived and conceived; it is a relation between him and ourselves. Hence it is possible for a person falsely to communicate though he has true knowledge. Perhaps it is because there is so much deception as well as error in communication that believing, this indirect relation to objects which is a direct relation to persons, is in our common speech associated with uncertainty. At all events what we acknowledge in all those acts of believing which are ingredient in our acts of knowing is the presence of moral subjects, that is, of persons, that is, of beings who live as self-binding, as promise-making, promise-keeping, promise-breaking, covenanting selves and never merely as knowers.

How much this believing as trusting in beings who keep faith, this disbelieving as distrusting of beings who break faith, this acknowledgment in either case of persons, enters into all our knowing the example of science in the modern world again makes clear. The word science represents to most men a great body of beliefs about objects of which they have no direct knowledge. But they hold these beliefs with great assurance because they trust the scientists. These have commended themselves to men as a group by the signs and miracles which "demonstrate the truth" of their ideas, or by the fulfillment of the predictions they have made, all of which seems to guarantee that their communications are without error. But even more they have invited confidence by the disinterestedness with which they have disciplined their tendency to deceive themselves, by the honesty with which they have confessed their ignorance, and the fidelity with which they have refrained from using their power as a way of exploiting other groups in their own interest. They are said to enjoy prestige in our society, but it may be better to say that they receive confidence and that this confidence rests on the double foundation of the acknowledgment that they are not deceived by the objective realities with which they deal and that they do not deceive their fellowmen. Wherever there is authority which is believed there is personality, singly or in groups, which is trusted as both knowing and as keeping faith, never merely as knowing.

Selves are social knowers who live in covenant relations. Such beings are known or acknowledged in our believing. Believing and the knowledge of beings of this sort belong together. Outside of such faith there is no knowledge of selves. In believing we not only act as selves but acknowledge the presence of other selves.

We are as yet a far cry from understanding the knowledge of God which is present in faith, but if these things be true of our ordinary believing, we are perhaps prepared to understand how social is our faith in God, how it includes acknowledgment of Him as faithful person, and also includes truth-relationship between selves and companions.

4

THE STRUCTURE OF FAITH

It is the characteristic of the situation in which we speak of faith that we need to communicate by means of parables, analogies and symbols. All communication is of this sort. We cannot help one another in the identification or understanding of some common object save by saying, "The thing to which I am directing your attention is something like this"; or "the feature of the common reality to which we are both attending but which I now ask you to observe more closely is analogous to this or that." This appears to be true of all communication about perceived objects, as when we inquire together into the form of a leaf and say to one another, "It is serrate," that is, sawlike, or "It is palmate" or "It is veined." It is especially true when we are dealing with realities that are not objects of sense perception, such as conscience, or the form of the state, or patriotism or human freedom. In the present instance we have apparently begun with such a parable. What we are speaking of, we have suggested, is like the relation of trusting and distrusting one another which is present when we seek to know any object; it is like that acknowledging of persons which is present in our believing and disbelieving of one another. Faith, however, as that subjective activity which is the counterpart of the objective God, without which God is not known as God, has not yet come into view.

Yet we begin to see that we are involved in more than analogical communication. Something is being assumed which must be acknowledged and brought into the agreement between the communicators, namely, the presence in our common life of a believing and trusting that is more than a believing and trusting and acknowledging one another. It is being assumed that this inquiry is being conducted in the company of "believers" who are not only in relations of trust and distrust to one another but in relations of trust and distrust to something beyond both, and who are aware of this fact and seek to understand this relation better. Hence we shall proceed on the basis of the agreement that we are not trying to persuade one another to believe in God, but rather to understand how it is that we believe and what knowledge there is in this believing. In this situation we are more or less consciously aware of the fact that our believing and disbelieving of each other is not only a parable of our believing and disbelieving God but is intimately connected with it. It is this whole into which we are inquiring and it is necessary as we do so that we state serially, in consecutive sentences, paragraphs and chapters, what presents itself to us as a whole with many parts.

Hence there must be agreement between the communicators that they will follow some kind of order in this serial presentation. Without such order, more or less arbitrarily chosen by the leader of an inquiry but assented to in some provisional manner by readers and hearers, no common analysis of even the simplest object in experience is possible. In trying to understand the tree which presents itself to us as the common object of our separate vision, we may agree to follow a spatial order, beginning with the branches and descending to the roots, or vice versa; we may choose a temporal order, beginning with the seed and following the course of the tree's development to decay, or vice versa; we may, as we do most frequently, follow a so-called logical order by moving from individual tree to its species, as elm, or pine, or cherry, from species to genus, and, if we are very curious, proceed thence to the category of life and to the idea of being. It is important in all such inquiries that it be agreed that some order be followed while it is recognized that this is not the only order, or the "true" order, but only an order of attention and communication. As we regard faith, a complex whole is present to us, some of it immediately in view to reflection, as in the common act of believing one another; some of it hidden for the moment. It is a temporal whole, which we can undertake to trace from its beginning, as do those theologies which begin with the first man and with the act of distrust that was the fall.[1] But when we make

1. See, for instance, Luther's Commentary on Genesis. This terse reference leaves it uncertain which version of Luther's commentary on Genesis the author em-

this historical beginning, we become aware of the fact that we have made our personal beginning with an act of believing the church or the Scriptures. Hence it appears that we may follow another order, namely the psychological order of Catholicism or of Protestantism. In this case we may begin with the believing of church or Scriptures as the first belief in our personal experience and try to trace out the order of faith by moving forward and backward to faith in God which is implied and which is furthered by belief in these, to the faith in nature and in our fellowmen, which is recognized in Scriptures and by the church and reinforced by them. This brings into view the possibility of following a third order which we may name the organic or social order in which the whole before us is a partly discerned structure of faith, the interpersonal order in which God and man, self and companion, Christ and the Father, Christ and the church, church and Scriptures, God and world are related to each other. It is such a complex structure of faith which rises into partial view as we direct our attention to the simple act of believing, yet we do so as those who have been included in the community of faith established or reestablished by Jesus Christ. This is the order of inquiry and of statement that we shall attempt to follow, an order which prevents us from saying that the "true" beginning of faith must be made by starting with Scriptures, or with the church, or with our relations to our companions. Rather we assume that we are dealing with a complex whole which is something like an organism, so that we must try to move in orderly fashion from point to point in our analysis, yet what we are doing is more like the work of an anatomist who seeks to dissect out of the body a complex nervous system than like the work of a logician who proceeds from *infima species* to *summum genus*.

Because of this methodology and the need for stating in succession what is presented to us simultaneously in our object, the presentation may have the appearance of an argument, as though we were attempting to persuade our companions in this inquiry to assent to inferences, to accept faith in God because of the presence of faith on earth, or to

---

ployed. Among the possibilities is *Dr. Martin Luthers Auslegung des ersten Buches Mosis*, ed. Th. Stiasny, 2 vols. (Leipzig: Gustav Lunkenbein, 1929). More recently, J. Theodore Mueller edited and translated *Luther's Commentary on Genesis*, 2 vols. (Grand Rapids, Michigan: Zondervan, 1958). [Editor's note.]

assent to the personal character of the Godhead because faith among humans is an acknowledgment of selfhood.[2] Where there is some faith in God, though it is much smaller than that mustard-seed faith of which Jesus spoke, it is impossible to abstract from its presence and to begin an inquiry as though it were not present. All human faith is now seen as connected with that faith. But what is seen is not only faith in God but a structure of faith, perverted, twisted and warped without a doubt, but nevertheless present. Hence though our order of inquiry calls for an analysis of faith that begins with its presence among men in their personal interrelations it does not or ought not pretend to be an order of inference or to be regarded as an effort to persuade those to acknowledge God in faith who do not do so. In the light of faith in God it appears that there was never a time when faith in Him was wholly absent from our existence though it was present in perverted and immature form; in the light of that faith it appears that images of and participations in it are present in all human existence, so that we are not dealing simply with parables but with participations of faith. If this be true then the inquiry of believers into their faith may be of help to those for whom faith in God in their own lives and the lives of others is an obscure and deceptive presence. But such faith is not established by inquiry or argument and hence our effort is not directed toward the conversion of unbelievers, if such there be, into believers, but toward the self-knowledge of believers.

THE first part of the structure of faith to which we attended is that interaction of self and other persons which appears in the act of believing the other. In this act of believing the I acknowledges the presence of a Thou. We find ourselves in the midst of that situation which in their different ways Martin Buber and G. H. Mead and their various followers have illumined for us. The self, they have pointed out, has

---

2. A. E. Taylor's *Faith of a Moralist* is an example of the sort of analysis we are here pursuing. If the first volume only of this work is read it appears to be an argument for the necessity of ascending from moral experience to religious faith, but when the second volume is taken into consideration it appears that religious faith has been presupposed as the basis for the sort of ethical experience with which the author seems to begin. When the whole work is read it is seen that the author has analyzed a complex whole, not argued from the known to the unknown.

a social character; it can know itself and be itself only as it confronts another knower who knows the self. "I" and "Thou" belong together. But in our analysis of the act of believing we have come upon the presence in this "I-Thou" situation of two elements which have perhaps not been sufficiently attended to in many of the observations made on the social nature of selfhood. The first of these is the presence to the "I" and the "Thou" of a third, of an *It*. There may be moments of intense awareness of self and other persons in which nothing appears to be present except the *I* and *Thou* knowing each other, but for the most part we know each other and ourselves as knowers, as knowing selves, only insofar as we have a common object. We have community with each other and can communicate with each other just because we are not only present to each other but have a common copresence, some object with which and about which we can communicate. Apart from such common objects we do not communicate but have only mutual awareness of or feeling for each other. *I, Thou* and *It* form a triad in such a way that all knowledge of the *It* depends on a self's relation to other selves; an *I* has no direct knowledge of the *It* without using the contributions of other selves who also have a direct relation to *It*. Nor does the *I* seem to have any direct relation to a *Thou* without reference to its relation to an object. I know you or acknowledge you in my act of believing your statements about a common third.

The second element in this "I-Thou" situation which has been brought to our attention and which seems not to have been adequately recognized in most of the observation made on this subject since Feuerbach's time is the *faith* relationship which is present between *I* and *Thou*. The self not only acknowledges the other as another knower but in believing and disbelieving him, it trusts or distrusts him as another self that has the double freedom of being able to bind itself by promises and yet to break them also. Faith is present here in the reciprocal action of *I* and *Thou* in which an *I* trusts a *Thou* and so acknowledges the latter as a person—one who has the fidelity-infidelity of moral personality. Trust is a response to and an acknowledgment of fidelity. The two are so interrelated in the reciprocal action of selves that one cannot speak of faith simply as the trust which appears but must speak of it also as the fidelity to which trust is the response. *Fides, fiducia* and *fidelitas* (to use the Latin words which have the advantage that they all represent variations of one root, as believing, trust and loyalty do

not) are not three different meanings of the word faith but three parts
of one interpersonal action in which *fides* (believing) is the phenome-
nal element which is largely based on the fundamental interaction of
fiducia (trust) and *fidelitas* (loyalty or fidelity).

As we have noted the fidelity which is trusted is that peculiar element in personality without which selves—though feeling, knowing
and desiring subjects—are not selves. It is the mode of self-existence
which comes to appearance in the making, keeping and breaking of
promises, in the acts of loyalty and treason of which selves are capable
and in which they exist. The self that I acknowledge in my act of trusting is a being that acts with a peculiar kind of freedom and under a
peculiar necessity. It has the freedom not only to attend to this or that
reality as knowing self, not only to choose this or that good as desiring
self, but to bind itself by promises, to choose goods that are not necessarily its own, to attend to beings in which it is not interested. It can
"swear to its own hurt and not change." It is a being that as marriage
companion has the freedom not only to say "I love you and so far as
I can predict I shall always love you" but rather, "I will honor, love
and keep you in sickness and in health, in prosperity and in adversity
and in every change of condition until death do us part." It is a being
that as companion-citizen can take an oath binding itself to administer
laws of the state without preference for its own values or to give up
its life for the sake of the community to which we both belong. It is a
being, such as my physician, who has explicitly or implicitly taken the
Hippocratic oath, promising: "The regimen I adopt shall be for the
benefit of my patients according to my ability and judgment, and not
for their hurt or for any wrong. . . . Whatsoever house I enter there
will I go for the benefit of the sick, refraining from all wrongdoing
or corruption. . . . Whatsoever things I see or hear concerning the life
of men in my attendance on the sick or even apart therefrom, which
ought not to be noised abroad, I will keep silence thereon, counting
such things to be as sacred secrets." It is a being that as my teacher,
my banker, my lawyer, my minister, has bound itself by explicit and
implicit agreements to "keep faith" with me. This is the freedom or an
aspect of the freedom of selves; yet selves are beings that are under the
necessity of exercising this freedom if they would be selves. Perhaps it
is better to say they are beings which have come to selfhood only as
they have exercised this freedom, for, as Josiah Royce has pointed out,

until a man has committed himself to a cause and taken such an oath or made such a promise he has not attained moral selfhood.[3]

This freedom has two other aspects. Though a self must make promises, enter into covenants, bind itself by its own action in order to be a self, yet it has freedom, within limits, to make one promise rather than another. It may take the vow of celibacy rather than that of marriage; it may make marriage-promises to one man or woman rather than to another; it may take the oath of the pacifist rather than that of the soldier, the vow of the public executioner rather than the Hippocratic oath, make the promises of the churchman rather than those of the statesman. Beyond this freedom there lies the further dreadful freedom of being able to break promises and violate trust. The self is the being which having come to selfhood in making commitments is at almost every moment free to become faithless, an adulterer, a corrupt politician, a traitor. The freedom of treason is the dark side of the freedom of fidelity. But the presence of treason is only the presence of loyalty or fidelity in its inverse form. For treason is not absence of fidelity; it does not exist where there are no covenants, and no selves, no trust in fidelity. It is the dark possibility of selfhood, not a possibility for beings which do not have the responsibility and the ability and necessity of fidelity. It is not unloyalty but disloyalty. It calls forth from other selves not mere uncertainty but distrust.

In the I-Thou relationship the interaction of trust and loyalty is reciprocal. As I trust and distrust the other loyal-disloyal self I become aware of myself as one trusted or distrusted by the other in my loyalty and disloyalty. It may be that for the most part the self endeavors to continue in a state of immaturity in which it trusts and distrusts others expecting them to be faithful while it is unwilling to accept itself as object of the other's trust and distrust or unwilling to reflect on its own commitments, loyalties and treasons. This seems to be the case in our political life where citizens full of distrust of their officials fail to raise the question of their own commitments, their own fidelity in

3. Royce develops the intimate connections between conscience and loyalty to a cause as constitutive of selfhood in *The Philosophy of Loyalty* (New York: Macmillan, 1908). He writes, for example, "[A] self is a life in so far as it is unified by a single purpose. Our loyalties furnish such purposes, and hence make us conscious and unified moral persons" (171). Royce carries his description and analysis further in *The Problem of Christianity*, published in 1913. [Editor's note.]

the discharge of their promises to one another, their own abuses of trust. This is the immaturity which appears in the marriage partner who seeks his own happiness and relies upon his mate to promote that happiness but fails to think of himself as committed to the promotion of the other's happiness. It is the immaturity of man in the presence of the Transcendent who makes God the object of his trust and distrust while he evades the question of his own fidelity to God. It is immaturity because it is the attitude of the child who has learned to acknowledge personality in the other without coming to recognition of himself as person, bound by promises and committed to the service of the other. Of course, more than immaturity is involved in most of these instances, for what is present is the effort to continue in the situation of childhood after in fact the privileges of maturity, the privileges of a freedom that has bound itself, have been claimed. Trust by the self in the other's faithfulness has as its necessary counterpart faithfulness in the self as that in which the other can in turn trust. The acceptance of promises made by the other to the self is at the same time an act of commitment in which the self agrees at the least to acknowledge the other as a person, in which it promises at least this much, that it will be grateful; for to be grateful is to recognize that what is received comes from personal freedom not from compulsion; it contains the acknowledgment of the other's selfhood. Entrance into personal relations with an other by the act of trust doubtless contains much more in the way of commitment and of promise making by the self, as when a student enters into a community where he accepts the promises of a company of teachers that they will inquire disinterestedly and communicate honestly and thereby implicitly promises not to deceive them in his communications to them. But it always contains this much, the promise to continue to acknowledge the other as a person.

Thus faith exists in the I-Thou community in the reciprocity of the trust and distrust which respond to fidelity and infidelity, shuttling back and forth between selves who have this peculiar nature that they cannot live as selves save in covenant relations.

As we regard this I-Thou relationship of persons who not only know each other as knowers but acknowledge each other as covenanting, promise-making free selves, we become aware of the fact that the community of faith, like the community of knowledge, is not a simple dyad. As in the community of the knowing I and the knowing Thou a third reality, the common object, is present, so in the community of faith a third reality besides I and Thou comes into view. We may for the present, with Josiah Royce, call this third reality a cause and note its presence in all the common covenant relations of men.

When student and teacher are related to each other as mature beings who trust each other and keep faith with each other they are at the same time acknowledging each other as selves who are bound to serve a cause which transcends both. The student has made a promise or bound himself not only to a teacher but to a host of inquirers and learners of many centuries, located in many places, who have all bound themselves to seek truth as well as to communicate truly. Truth here is a vague word which designates the common cause. It is something that is objective to, separate from, all these subjects who, bound to each other in trust and fidelity, are also devoted or bound to something that is not in the community. It is that for the sake of which the community exists, for the sake of which all these I's and Thou's are united. What is this third reality? Is it simply a larger community? The university community as a We-group is aware of the fact that it has entered into relations of faith with other communities, such as those of church and nation, with implicit promises that it will not deceive them nor seek in the performance of its own special function in the service of its cause to make itself powerful over them. But this larger faith-community is not the specific cause which the university community, in all its special embodiments, is united in serving. It has bound itself, and each self that enters into it binds himself, to the specific cause of knowing "the Truth" and serving "the Truth." What the nature of this cause called "Truth" is may be subject to dispute. For one kind of value theorist it is an objective value, an "ought-to-be," that lays claim on men; for another, the pragmatist, it is an instrumental value which must be sought for the sake of promoting life, but even he recognizes that science must forget about the instrumental value of truth and often be completely pure and disinterested if it is to become practical in the end. The term "Truth" stands for a cause which is something more therefore than the personal value of all the members of the community of truth seekers bound to each other by promises to speak truth to each other; it also stands for more than the personal value of all the persons in all other communities to whom the community of truth-seekers is related by faith, that is, by promises of loyalty to them. Unless this third, the cause, is present the I-Thou relationship of fellow-students or of teachers and students in the enterprise of learning is debauched into a sophistic enterprise of mutual career promoting, or it may become a nationalistic or communistic enterprise which serves a larger community but not "Truth."

We notice the presence of the third element, the cause, in the reciprocity of trust and loyalty of fellow-citizens of a nation. As faithful fellow-citizens they maintain each other in their rights, claim for the other the same equitable administration of laws which they desire for themselves, seek to forget their likes and dislikes of each other in their effort to keep their promises to each other that each shall have fair trial if accused of crime, that each shall respect the conscience of the other in the exercise of his personal duties, and so forth. Yet they are not bound to each other in simple reciprocity of fidelity and trust. For each of them must also trust the other to be faithful to the common cause. And that common cause is not only the structure of laws, or the community itself as including not only these mutually engaged citizens but their fathers and their posterity as well; the common cause is indeed a nation which has bound itself to its members by the promises in the laws; but it has also bound itself to serve in its common life a cause that transcends the whole community, for the sake of which the community exists. On the one hand, this cause seems, as in the case of the university community, to be an abstract value to which an abstract name, in this case perhaps "Justice," must be given. On the other hand, as in the case of modern nation states, the cause is some particular value which is thought to be important to all men, not simply to the members of the nation—such a cause as "Freedom" or "Equality." The cause of the individual citizens who are bound to each other in faith relations is thus, on the one hand, the nation to which all are bound by promises; on the other hand, however, it is that cause to which the nation has bound itself, for the sake of which it believes that it exists. And this cause to which the nation has bound itself is never merely the larger community, for instance, the society of all nations, but some "form of good" which ought to be embodied, which ought to be realized, not only in its own life but in that of all other men.

In these two instances the third reality which appears to be necessary to a community of faith between an I and a Thou seems to be ultimately something that can only be designated by a concept; it is a form, a value, a supercommunal good which is acknowledged as a good for all men, not only for the members of the community which directly serves it. In the case of other communities of faith the cause is more concrete. Thus the marriage-community is completed by the coming of the third, a child, to which father and mother are now united, not by their loyalty to each other only, but by their direct loyalty to it, which in turn strengthens their loyalty to each other, since they now promise to each other that they will be loyal to the common object of devotion.

The triadic character of faith community as one which involves besides reciprocal trust and fidelity loyalty to a common cause becomes most apparent in the case of desertion and of treason. In desertion the cause is betrayed when the companion is deserted; in treason the companion is betrayed with the betrayal of the cause. The traitor is first disloyal to the common cause and thereby disloyal to his companions who trusted him and relied not only on his loyalty to them but to the cause in whose service they were united. His action is distinctly different from that of the neutral person who has never bound himself to the common cause. It is very different also from that of the enemy who has bound himself to an opposing cause. The traitor has broken his promise to the cause and therewith broken his promises to his companions; he is a betrayer of his community; but he is to be distinguished from the denier who has also failed to keep his promise to his companions because the denier breaks his promise to serve the cause in being faithless to the companion—while the traitor willfully breaks his promise to his companions that he will serve the cause and willfully abandons that commitment which is a part of his very existence as a self. In treason the commitment to the cause is abandoned and in consequence the commitment to the fellow-devotees of the cause is given up; in desertion, on the other hand, the companion is forsaken and in consequence the cause is abandoned. It is characteristic of the traitor that he seeks to keep the trust of his companions as one faithful to a cause in order that he may destroy the cause while the deserter makes no pretenses. In all our efforts in moral and legal judgment to deal adequately with treason, desertion, we make these distinctions.

Frequently, at least in recent times, the effort has also been made to explain treason to a cause by means of distrust in the companions.[4] Here the triadic relation seems to be recognized.

The triadic character of a faith community is brought to our attention in still another way when we reflect on the varieties of human association. The term community does not always mean faith-community; not all common life involves faith. Men are social beings in their physical, biological and intellectual life as well as in their existence as selves. Men are related to each other at different levels of their existence as those sociologists have discerned who have made an important distinction between the two kinds of human societies which they have named associations and communities. They have discovered and called attention to the great difference between "an organization of social beings . . . for the pursuit of some common interest or interests" and the "intense living together of men which makes a village or city or country" and which brings it about that the "beings who live together shall resemble each other," developing "in some kind and degree distinctive common characteristics—manners, traditions, modes of speech and so on."[5] Associations of the former sort are organizations such as Chambers of Commerce, labor unions, The Society for the Prevention of Cruelty to Animals, political parties, Union Leagues, the Ku Klux Klan, and so forth; communities of the latter type are represented by New England villages, Swiss cantons, the Russian people and Western civilization. One may define associations as societies in which relations are external to the terms related and communities as societies in which the relations are internal. In the former type of grouping individual members are not significantly changed by their relationship; in the latter they are, as when the traditions, language and customs of a family mold the mind and character of each of its members. Or, it may be pointed out, associations are organizations of interests rather than of men, for each individual in the association tends to function in that setting as an interest or set of interests rather than

4. See Rebecca West, *The Meaning of Treason* (New York: Viking, 1947).
5. R. M. Maciver, *Community: A Sociological Study* (London: Macmillan, 1920), 23f. See also Ferdinand Toennies, *Gemeinschaft und Gesellschaft* (Leipzig: R. Reisland, 1887).

as a whole man. Communities, on the other hand, are organizations of men in their larger reality as psycho-physical beings.

A further distinction must be made, however, and one which sociology cannot well make insofar as it seeks to confine itself to the interpretation of what can be externally observed in social behavior. This is the distinction between communities of human individuals and communities of selves. A community in the sociological sense is not necessarily a community in what, for want of a better term, we may call a spiritual sense, using the word spirit here to mean selfhood. There is a genuine and intelligible difference between a society in which *selves* are associated in common fidelity, respect and responsibility and a community of the sort described above, as well as between such a spiritual society and an association. To be sure, it is often difficult to discover an exact line of demarcation between one sort of society and another. Neither is it possible to classify the various groups we find in our experience so as to assign families, nations, unions, and so forth to one or the other category. The differences are partly differences of degree but even more of levels of existence.

Marriage communities may be taken as illustrations of the three sorts of society mentioned above. A union of man and woman may be an association formed for the sake of pursuing common interests. The two may marry for the sake of mutual sexual satisfaction, the propagation of children, economic or cultural advantages. It is often emphasized by those who regard all marriages as associations of this sort that the union is more likely to be enduring if the common interests are numerous. But whether they be few or many such marriage is an association into which individuals enter with little expectation of changing their patterns of thought and conduct in any fundamental manner. The relations remain largely external to the terms related, or the terms related are not so much whole individuals as sets of interests. A marriage, however, may be a society in the second sociological sense defined above. Among the motives which have led to its beginning the desire for complete community of life with the other rather than the satisfaction of special interests may have been prominent. Intense living together may establish a similarity between husband and wife so that they speak the same language down to fine nuances of meaning, so that they think on the basis of the same premises and arrive at the same conclusions, have like tastes and scales of values, share a common memory and a common hope.[6] The relations in this case are internal in the sense that the related terms are profoundly changed by being brought into relation. What is related, however, is not interests so much as interested individuals.

There is, however, a third possibility in marriage. Husband and wife may be united on the basis of common commitment to each other as selves in a covenant, which is far more inclusive than a contract to serve each other in the pursuit of common interests and, however much of common life it may involve, never results in the merging of personalities into a kind of whole. The marriage union will be characterized by mutual respect for each other as responsible selves, independent of each other yet bound to each other in trust and responsibility. The respect for each other may be associated with common but also with divergent interests. Common interests indeed are present in such a marriage as are common memories and common hopes and intense living together, but the marriage union has also been established at another level, so that it remains in effect even when these elements are diminished or even destroyed. Responsibility to each other and for each other as selves, concern for each other's good even when it is not obviously a common good, in short, *faithfulness* or *fidelity* constitutes the bond in such a marriage.

The distinction between the three kinds of marriage is not a difference of degrees of association. There may, indeed, be progress from one type to another, as when association issues in community, or when persons who enter into marriage immaturely, without responsibility as selves and without understanding of the partner's selfhood, grow into maturity, surrender their possessiveness and egocentrism and substitute honor, respect, trust and fidelity to the other for self-interestedness. There may be a movement from community of mind to community of selves also, as when a patriarchal family, in which intense living together promotes similarity of manners, customs and ideas, develops into an egalitarian family, in which there is less common life but more responsibility, independence, respect and fidelity

6. The importance for community of common memory and common hope has been emphasized by Josiah Royce, especially in his *Problem of Christianity*, 2 vols. (New York: Macmillan, 1913) vol. 2, chapters 9 and 10.

among the members. The three types, it is evident, do not represent *degrees* of intimacy or closeness, but rather *sorts* of intimacy. There is a gap between the stages, a leap is required in passing from the one to the other. In the last instance it is a leap of faith. The differences are due not to the relationships between the terms only but to the nature of the terms related—*interests, minds or selves.*[7]

The same distinctions must be made in the case of political societies. It is as erroneous to try to describe the state as either an association or a community as it is to do this in the case of marriage and family societies. The state may be an association, limited to the promotion of certain specified ends, such as the protection of individuals living in a certain area against internal disorder and external aggression. The Jeffersonian conception of the state and the Jeffersonian state, for instance, is associationist. The state may also be a community, as in the case of the modern nation state, which represents and expresses the common life of men who have common speech, common traditions, customs, memories and hopes. But a state, in the third place, may be a society of responsible selves who are faithful to each other as selves and faithful also to a common cause which transcends their individual interests in life, liberty and the pursuit of happiness. What has been ignored in the long debate about the natural or contractual character of the state has often been this third element, for the *covenant of selves with selves has been confused with the contracts interested individuals make with other interested individuals for the sake of limited ends.* Doubtless there are no states which are of a purely covenant character as there are no families into which common interest and common mind do not enter. But when covenant is added to interest the nature of a society is transformed so that interest plays a less important role than before. Community of mind also may be transformed by the appearance of responsibility, as in the gradual development of what we call democracies out of old national communities, with their patriarchal, kingly organization. These changes imply not so much changes of relation between beings who remain constant as changes in the beings related, for men enter into covenant and relations of fidelity as responsible selves who bind themselves to others and to a common cause,

7. See Fritz Kunkel, *In Search of Maturity* (New York: Charles Scribner's Sons, 1944), 69ff., 187ff.

whereas they participate in associations as bundles of interest and in communities of mind as consciousnesses.

The community which is the counterpart of faith and responsibility is like an association insofar as it is based on choice rather than on nature, on an act of freedom rather than of fate. It is like a natural community insofar as its relations are internal, since one cannot remain true to one's self if one is untrue to those to whom one is related in responsibility. It is unlike an interest association in that the origin of the choice does not lie in an interest in a thing, a feeling or anything that can be possessed; the chooser is the self and what is chosen is another self or community of selves not as possession but as partner to whom one will be responsible.

Now it seems evident that when an association or a community becomes such a faith-society what is present is always a third reality as a common cause. The husband who respects his wife as a person, and does not only love her as an associate with common interests including an interest in himself or participate with her in common memories and hopes, respects her as a being who has an independent relation to a cause or to causes. He is loyal to her and loyal to her loyalties. He recognizes that she is one who has a loyalty which takes precedence over her loyalty to him; she is one who must keep faith not only with him but with something that transcends them both. The citizen who has come to maturity and has entered into faith relations with his fellow-citizens honors and respects them even in the clash of opinions about what is for the interest of each and for the common interests, for he is aware that the fellow-citizen has a loyalty that is more important than his fidelity to the companion. When societies become societies of selves in which men bind themselves to each other as selves who will be faithful to each other there is always present some third reality beyond the I and Thou to which I and Thou have their direct relationship.

Is something more to be said about these third realities which seem to be necessary elements in every genuine community of selves with selves? We can define them simply as the objects of loyalty, that is, as the causes to which I's and Thou's bind themselves to be faithful at the same time that they bind themselves to each other by acts of loyalty and trust.

On the one hand such a common object of loyalty is an intrinsic good to which the self and its companions are bound not only by their oath of loyalty but by the claim which it makes upon them for their loyalty. It is something which obligates and not only something to which in freedom one obligates oneself. This is true when it is a concrete good, such as the child in the family which by its coming obligates both father and mother, while at the same time they obligate themselves to it in the continuous acts of decision to acknowledge the child as their very own. It is also true when the common object of loyalty is designated by an abstract term such as truth or justice, for truth and justice represent powers—whether as essential values or otherwise —which lay claim upon selves so that the loyalty which the self directs to them is a kind of answer to a demand which issues from them. This is the point which all objective value theorists make and it is hard to avoid agreeing with them however skeptical one may be about their observations concerning the ontological status of such values. There is a certain reciprocity here between the loyal selves and the cause; the movement of loyalty is not entirely from self to cause; there is a movement from cause to self, a movement which has something of the nature of a claim or demand.

Again we observe that such a cause is not only an object of loyalty but to a certain extent an object of trust. The community of men who are loyal to justice and loyal to each other in their common fidelity to justice, also depend upon something in the nature of justice or in the nature of the world not to let them down. There is a trust here that devotion to justice will not result in futility. There is trust that the companions in the service of justice will not become victims of deceit. So it is with truth. The community of those who are devoted to the cause of truth live in the trust that this service is not a futile thing which will ultimately make loyal servants of truth appear to be fools, and that the service of truth will not be inimical to all the other good causes to which men devote their lives. It is at this point that the conflict of the university with the interest associations of the modern world arises. For behind the university there is the trust that if truth be sought the other values in which men are interested will not be imperiled, while the interest associations of men live in the constant fear that what the universities are seeking is not truth but the power of some special group or that if truth be made the cause of devotion than national life or wealth or even religious security will be lost. Trust also appears in the case of the child as the common object of parental loyalty. Not that the child as such is primarily the object of trust, though it is also trusted where the loyalty is great. But what is trusted is some reality connected with the child; a reality which will not only bring the child eventually to respect the parents rather than to use them as mere instruments of its own interests but a reality which will conserve the child, which will unite this cause of parental loyalty with all other enduring causes.

The third element in the community of loyalty and trust is thus not only an object of loyalty but an object of trust, since trust is always an ingredient in the relation of the loyal selves to it. This third element cannot be simply identified with the community of the loyal, since this community always has an object beyond itself for the sake of which it exists. It is intimately connected with the community, as when the citizens of the state are loyal to the whole community and the members of the community of truth seekers are loyal to all who are united with them. But the cause transcends any community of selves. No matter how large the We-group of the loyal grows that which unites them in loyalty is always something beyond the community for the sake of which they are united in community. Neither can we identify the transcendent object of loyalty, as Royce does, with loyalty itself, since loyalty relates one to a cause and in any form in which it is conceivable points beyond itself to something that transcends it.

When we have inquired thus far into the structure of faith there appears on the horizon the mystery of the Transcendent. It seems that even when we deal with the structures of faith as we find them in our ordinary experience we are dealing with realities that point beyond themselves to a cause beyond all causes, to an object of loyalty beyond all concrete persons and abstract values, to the Being or the Ground of Being which obligates and demands trust, which unites us in universal community. In the light of Christian faith this is evidently so. The structures of faith which we find in our world are not only shadows and images of divine things but participate in the ultimate structure. Behind the faiths and communities of faith in which we are united in family and nation and company of scholars there looms the grand structure of a community of faith which is universal, in which all selves are involved as companions and in which the third, the cause and object of trust, is the transcendent reality, present wherever two or three are present to each other or anyone is present to himself. This structure, to be sure, rises into view only in broken form; as a structure in which faith in its negative aspects as disloyalty and distrust comes to appearance more frequently than in its positive form. But though in ruined form yet there are evidences of its presence in all our existences as faithful-unfaithful selves.

As we have reflected on faith we have come to see that it is no merely subjective experience. When it appears in the subject it appears as the response to and acknowledgment of another person who like the self exists in trust and loyalty. Faith, selfhood and other-self are insepa- rable. Moreover the presence of faith in life, whether in its positive or negative form, always represents the acknowledgment of something personal in the Transcendent. The reality of selfhood or, to use the good old fashioned term, of the soul, comes to appearance in the ac- tivity of trusting and distrusting, being loyal and deceiving. The reality of an other self is acknowledged, depended upon in the act of trusting and distrusting, being faithful to him and deceiving him. The reality of God, of the Transcendent One, is obscurely acknowledged in life's distrust and anxiety and openly so in trust in Him, loyalty to Him and loyalty to the objects of his loyalty. The certainty of faith may be stated in a somewhat Cartesian fashion: I believe (i.e., trust-distrust, swear allegiance and betray) therefore I know that I am, but also I trust you and therefore I am certain that you are, and I trust and distrust the Ultimate Environment, the Absolute Source of my being, therefore I acknowledge that He is. There are three realities of which I am cer- tain, self, companions and the Transcendent. I assume the reality of these three even when I communicate my doubts to another. For to speak a word or to write a sentence is to acknowledge the presence of another person who trusts and distrusts me, and it is to affirm "I am here as one who wills not to deceive." And since it is a word or a sen- tence about a third reality, it is an acknowledgment of something that transcends the self and the other to whom I communicate. And in this acknowledgment of a transcendent object there is included acknowl- edgment of an Absolute. If "I" say to "Thee," "This color which we see is purely subjective; it would not be there if you and I were not there,"

I am affirming something about the nature of things, about that which has made you and me and our objective world as they are, and I am saying also that I distrust it. The acceptance and the acknowledgment of personal reality is the fact from which we abstract in our communications but which is always present, always assumed. The movement of life is not from idea to personality but personality to idea.

5

BROKEN FAITH

So far we have described the nature of faith in formal and abstract manner. We have noted, in the first place, that faith is a peculiar kind of subjective activity intimately connected with our existence as selves. Faith and personality belong together. To be a self is to be the kind of being which can and must bind itself by promises to other selves; which must keep faith with others; which in this I-Thou relationship of loyal-disloyal promise makers trusts and distrusts. Thus not only faith and personality but faith and the interpersonal nature of personal existence are correlative. Further, we have noted, faith is present in the triadic structure of our interpersonal society. We are bound to each other in trust and loyalty only as we are mutually bound to some third reality, to a cause, to which both "I" and "Thou" owe loyalty and on which both depend. We can and do believe each other because we recognize in each other a loyalty which is more than mutual promise keeping.

As we arrive at this point there seems to arise into view the possibility of moving toward the idea of a universal cause. We are tempted to reflect that as human beings we are bound to each other not only in various special societies with their special causes but universally, so that we recognize in each other beyond all special ties a common loyalty and a common bond. It is suggested to us that there may be here an argument for the presence of God as the universal cause, or that a form of the ontological argument for God has come to appearance in the recognition that the idea of a universal cause is given with our existence as moral men, that is, as men who are moral in this particular sense: we are, by necessity and in freedom, beings that are bound to a cause and bound to each other. However we are warned against the effort of seeking to develop a "pistological" argument for the existence of God by the reflection that it is impossible for us so to abstract from our actual faith as to pretend that in moving from the familiar ground of ordinary personal loyalties to faith in God we are moving from the known to the unknown.[1] If the theologian undertakes to do what the philosopher does he is not keeping faith with those to whom he is speaking for he counts himself a member of the community of faith in God. In his own thinking he is not moving from known to unknown when he moves from man's faith in man to man's faith in God; he is rather seeking to understand one known by means of another known. Moreover he is aware of the fact that faith in God is not for him an inference, nor has it been established by inference. Hence, however much he may feel that others ought to recognize that the reality of human faith implies the existence of the God of faith, he also recognizes that the implication is probably clear to him because he knows this faith in God to begin with; he sees how it is involved in everything else in human existence. His method therefore must always be the method of confession and demonstration. Theology is an effort to understand a faith that has been given, not an effort to understand in order that we may believe.

Our procedure therefore must be this, that we now use the understanding we have gained of the general structure of faith in interpersonal life for the sake of analyzing, as best we may, that faith in God of which we are conscious in ourselves in the company of the faithful. What we become aware of first of all when we direct our attention to it is that it has always been present to us in a negative form and is now so present to us. Faith in God is the accompaniment of our existence as selves but first of all it is a dark background; it is present negatively as distrust and fear and hostility.

When the self conceives some trust in that God in whom Jesus

---

1. *Pistological*—this word may have been coined by the author. I have not encountered it elsewhere. It is formed on the base *pistis,* the word usually translated as *faith* in the New Testament but occasionally also as *faithfulness;* see, for example, Karl Barth's treatment of it in Rom. 1:17 and 3:22, 28 in his *Epistle to the Romans,* trans. E. C. Hoskyns (London: Oxford University Press, 1933). It is structurally analogous to the familiar term *epistemological,* formed on the base *episteme,* that is, knowledge. In various handwritten notes the author also occasionally uses *pistology.* [Editor's note.]

Christ trusted as Father, it becomes aware of the fact that it had always known of His presence though in such fashion that He was not acknowledged or recognized as God. We are accompanied in all our personal existence by the existence of other selves. Each I has its Thou's which it acknowledges immediately. But each self facing its companions in relations of trust and distrust, of loyalty and faithlessness, is also aware of that last reality on which both it and the other are dependent. It is aware, as Schleiermacher pointed out, of its absolute dependence; but it would be better to say, that it is aware of the Absolute on which it and its companions are dependent.[2] This transcendent reality, this last fact, this unconditioned, is no thing among things; it is no visible or conceptual reality. It is the inescapable, the radical source of self-existence, of the being of selves in time and place among other selves. Our existence as selves in this place and time comes home to us as the inexplicable event. Here we are, "thrown into existence," fated to be.[3] How far our freedom may modify the qualities of our existence we do not know; we know we have some freedom, but our freedom is not our beginning. One thing we understand perfectly and that is that we did not elect ourselves into being and that however we may change the qualities of our bodies or of our minds, this self which lives in this body and this mind did not choose itself. We recognize also that we do not have the freedom not to be, though we have the dreadful freedom of killing our bodies. If it is so that our selves continue after physical death then we can do nothing about it. So the fear of Hamlet lies on every free man who contemplates his own death—"but in that sleep of death what dreams may come?" (III, i) It is not in the control

2. See Friedrich Schleiermacher, *The Christian Faith*, trans. H. R. Mackintosh and J. S. Stewart (Edinburgh: T and T Clark, 1928). In proposition 4, Schleiermacher defines religion or *piety* as "the consciousness of being absolutely dependent, or, which is the same thing, of being in relation with God." [Editor's note.]

3. The phrase "thrown into existence" seems to echo the language of Martin Heidegger. However, HRN penciled "Santayana" in the margin of the manuscript at this point, and indeed much in this paragraph, especially the emphasis on unfreedom, reflects the author's affinity with George Santayana, whose "Ultimate Religion" he often quoted. See *The Philosophy of Santayana*, ed. Irwin Edman (New York: Modern Library, n.d.). *Omnificent,* for example, which HRN uses below in this chapter, is a word coined by Santayana. [Editor's note.]

of the self to put an end to itself, as it was not in its control to begin itself. We are in the grip of power that neither asks our consent before it brings us into existence nor asks our agreement to continuing us in being beyond our physical death. Sooner or later we awake to the realization that this is the way things are. "I," "here," "now"—these are the dimensions or qualities of our unchosen, our unfree being, our existence as beings conditioned by that which transcends and conditions all other conditioning forces, such as nature, our families, and so forth.

In our existences as selves, in our unfree freedom, we are in the presence of that which determines us. The determination goes far beyond our bare existence as selves in this time and with these companions. We not only are but we are thus and so and it is difficult to define the limits between the action of the self, the action of other powers and the actions of the last reality in making us thus and so save in this one bare fact of selfhood in this time. Yet we are aware of the presence of that which is transcendent, unconditioned, all-conditioning not only as we face the riddle of our individual selfhood. It is brought home to us in our meeting with our alter egos, those other selves without whom we do not exist. Let the parent think of his child, involved in tragedy; let the statesman think of the citizens of the nation for which he bears responsibility, and he must think of them in relation to that transcendent and unconditioned reality which has brought these beings into this existence in this time. It is not in speculations about First Cause or Final End that the awareness of the transcendent principle of determination comes upon us. When we regard the world of things impersonally there is no reason why we should not pursue our inquiries ad infinitum from present to antecedent beyond antecedent, or to consequent beyond consequent. Our "natural" religion is not one of wonder about the source of natural things, whatever be the natural religion of primitive tribes. Our natural religion is inseparable from our existence as selves among selves. Here in the encounter of the "I" with that mystery of power which has thrown it into existence and confronted it with these other selves, here in the presence of the wonder appearing in the question of the child and of the aged, "Why am I here?" the awareness of the ultimate fact dawns upon us. There is a power or a structure or a form of reality here which cannot be changed. There is that here which we are up against. We have no name for it. As soon as we begin to analyze it we think of that which it evidently is not—the structure of nature or the pattern of natural forces. It is not this, for from this no self comes, only a body and a mind. From this the self can free itself in death, but it cannot emancipate itself from the ground of its being as self. One thing I seem to know: I am I in this now and I am up against that which has matched me with this time and this time with me, I am up against *that which is,* and without which I am not.

The self's relation to the Transcendent or the Unconditioned or the Enveloping is personal. It is the relation of a self which has become aware of its I-ness in the presence of its responsibility to Thou's. It is personal also in the sense that it is a relation of faith to the Transcendent. But we are immediately aware of this faith in its negative not its positive form, not as trust but as distrust, not as belief but as disbelief of what this Transcendent means to the self.

Our natural faith, our ordinary human attitude toward the transcendent source of our existence, is one of disappointment, of distrust, and of disbelief. In this very distrust is an acknowledgment of someone there; it is a personal attitude and it is directed toward something personal or it personalizes that toward which it is directed. Doubtless there is error in the statement that we "personalize" the Transcendent. To speak in this fashion is to confess that we have prejudices in favor of impersonal categories, as though the impersonal were more likely to characterize existence than the personal, as though thinghood were more original than selfhood and as though reification of the personal were not as great a source of error as the personalization of things. But our existential concern as selves, facing that which we are up against, the reality of being and being-thus-and-so, of self and its world, does not express itself in metaphysical inquiry to begin with. To begin with it does not turn to questions about the Transcendent, whether it is personal or not. That comes later and at another level of our consciousness. Our fundamental attitude, however, is personal; it is directed toward the Transcendent as personal; and it is ordinarily or naturally the attitude of distrust toward a being which in that act of distrust is acknowledged as being that ought to be loyal, yet is not.

This "natural" or "fallen" religion of ours has never yet yielded so completely to the converting influence of the gospel that it cannot be examined in the context of Christianity as well as of paganism. In seeking to understand it we are not only trying to reconstruct man's relation to the Transcendent prior to the advent of Jesus Christ or to remember our own relation to God prior to the slow or sudden communication of the faith of Jesus Christ to us in our new self-aware selfhood. We are trying to understand something in our present life, an old relation that may be passing away but which is nevertheless present. If such a venture seems highly confessional it is so not only in an individualistic but also in a communal sense since the evidences of the presence of this natural religion of negative faith are to be discovered not only in ourselves but in our companions, in their express statements as well as in their symbolic behavior.

"T H E mind of the flesh," says Paul, "is enmity to God" (Rom. 8:7).[4] We may state the thought more abstractly for the moment by saying that our natural, though not our fundamental, human relation to the Transcendent is one of distrust toward what is conceived to be deceptive, a distrust which appears in hostility, fear and isolation. These three forms are not wholly separable though in certain instances one or the other seems to prevail and to give a dominant tone to life in faithlessness. Sometimes defiance marks the human attitude in man's encounter with the ultimate antagonist; more frequently the sense of antagonism appears in the form of human fear before the powerful enemy and perhaps still more frequently the effort is made to put all thought of that Other out of the mind while the self devotes itself to the little struggles and victories of life. All three attitudes may be present in each individual, though publicly they are usually expressed by different individuals.

Overt expression of hostility by the self toward the Transcendent, the Determiner of Destiny, is relatively rare. When it is uttered in society the fearsomeness associated with the second form seeks at once to repress it, lest the Transcendent be moved to greater wrath against men. When it arises within the self a similar process of repression takes place. Basic to such hostility is the sense of profound

4. On HRN's quoting of Scripture see chapter 1, note 21. [Editor's note.]

disillusionment, of broken promise which has often been expressed in literature and which in these expressions vibrates answering strings in human sentiment. This disillusionment is present in the sermon in James Thomson's "The City of Dreadful Night." It is the mood we find in Edward Fitzgerald's "Omar Khayyam."[5] One finds it reflected in Joseph Conrad's novels.[6] It is echoed in music, at least as artistic perception hears music. So E. M. Forster describes Beethoven's Fifth Symphony in his *Howards End*.[7] It receives a dreadful expression in Shakespeare's *King Lear*:

> As flies to wanton boys, are we to the gods;
> They kill us for their sport. (IV, i)

But this disillusionment is not yet defiant hostility. The latter appears with immature boastful boldness, like that of William Ernest Henley in his "Invictus," when it is based on the sense of man's strength:

> Beyond this place of wrath and tears
> Looms but the horror of the shade,

---

5. At this point in the manuscript HRN quotes from "The City of Dreadful Night" and from "The Rubaiyat of Omar Khayyam." Since his own text and the other sources he introduces in this vicinity make his point sufficiently clear, I have omitted the stanzas. [Editor's note.]

6. The author here refers to "Day's Essays and note from Conrad's correspondence." I have not been able to identify this reference. The following lines in an 1898 letter from Conrad to R. B. Cunninghame Graham are, however, apposite to HRN's allusion to Conrad. "The mysteries of a universe made of drops of fire and clods of mud do not concern us in the least. The fate of a humanity condemned ultimately to perish from cold is not worth troubling about. If you take it to heart it becomes an unendurable tragedy. . . . Faith is a myth and beliefs shift like mists on the shore. . . . As our peasants say: 'Pray, brother, forgive me for the love of God.' And we don't know what forgiveness is, nor what is love, nor where God is" (*The Indispensable Conrad*, ed. M. D. Zabel [New York: The Book Society, 1951], 734f.). [Editor's note.]

7. In chapter 5 of *Howards End*, Forster describes Helen's thoughts as they move between a sense of "the splendour of life" and a premonition of the falling "ramparts of the world," while she listens to the third movement of the symphony. [Editor's note.]

> And yet the menace of the years
> Finds, and shall find me, unafraid.[8]

It appears in wiser and more tragic form when it is based on love
of fellowmen, victims of life's apparent cruelty or heedlessness. This
Promethean motif in natural religion does not arise out of the simple
confrontation of the self with Transcendence, with the Unconditioned,
with the determination of destiny. It arises rather out of the triadic
situation in which a self bound to other human selves in loyalty raises
its voice against Omnipotence on behalf of others. Perhaps in this
form Promethean defiance occurs only within the Christian context,
for it is a notable fact that where the problem of suffering is dealt
with in the Old Testament it is fundamentally a problem of the self's
suffering, not of its neighbor's. Even Job suffers in himself and not in
the sufferings of his children or his wife. This seems also to be the
case in those Psalms which deal with the problem. In Greek tragedy
the motif of sympathy seems also lacking. However that may be, the
Promethean motif of hostility as we have it in Shelley and Bertrand
Russell is inseparable from loyalty to one's fellowmen. Shelley's Prometheus "would fain Be . . . The savior and the strength of suffering
man."[9] His suffering is vicarious in the sense that it is occasioned by
his love of others. Out of that solidarity with men he hurls defiance
against the one

> Who fillest with thy soul this world of woe,
> To whom all things of Heaven and Earth do bow
> In fear and worship; all-prevailing foe![10]

8. William Ernest Henley (1849–1903) wrote "Invictus" during a prolonged period
of hospitalization in Edinburgh. [Editor's note.]

9. Percy Bysshe Shelley, "Prometheus Unbound," act 1, lines 816–17. Shelley's
Prometheus speaks on behalf of those whom Jove, "Monarch of Gods and Dae-
mons," has made his "multitudinous . . . slaves" and whose "knee-worship" he
requites, "With fear and self-contempt and barren hope" (act 1, lines 1–8). See
also act 1, lines 807–08: "and yet I feel Most vain all hope but love." [Editor's
note.]

10. "Prometheus Unbound," act 1, lines 283–85. These lines are spoken by the
"Phantasm of Jupiter," whom Prometheus petitions, "Speak the words which I
would hear" (line 248). [Editor's note.]

Bertrand Russell, among contemporary philosophers, has stated something like this same attitude of hostility. We must note, however, that when he states it he denies that he is speaking philosophically, since philosophy has as such no knowledge of self nor of anything personal which the self confronts in its world. As a philosopher he says, "I think that the external world may be an illusion, but if it exists, it consists of events, short, small and haphazard." [11] "The universe as known to science is not in itself either friendly or hostile to man." [12] As a world of events it may be described by means of a kind of "chrono-geography," which, however, Russell concedes, would be quite uninteresting. But the philosopher is also a living person with an ethical attitude as a self. "I did not write *Social Reconstruction*," says Russell, "in my capacity as a 'philosopher'; I wrote it as a human being who suffered from the state of the world, wished to find some way of improving it, and was anxious to speak in plain terms to others who had similar feelings. . . . If the book is to be understood my technical activities must be forgotten." [13] As such a man, as a self, which will not be "serene and above the battle," Russell gives utterance to the Promethean note of hostility toward the Transcendent. In his early "A Free Man's Worship" he described the actual world man confronts as not only indifferent to value but as hostile to it, as Power which is bad, a tyrant Fate which the free man can only defy with "Promethean constancy." [14] Though later he regarded this statement as over-solemn yet he repeated it in essence in *The Scientific Outlook*, in which he wrote that no comfort is "to be derived from the supposition that this very unpleasing universe was manufactured of set purpose." More than that, he goes on to say that

if indeed the world in which we live has been produced in accordance with a Plan, we shall have to reckon Nero a saint in com-

11. Bertrand Russell, *The Scientific Outlook* (New York: W. W. Norton, 1931), 98.

12. Bertrand Russell, *Philosophy* (New York: W. W. Norton, 1927), 301.

13. P. A. Schilpp, ed., *The Philosophy of Bertrand Russell* (Evanston, Ill.: Library of Living Philosophers, 1946), 730f.

14. "A Free Man's Worship" first appeared in 1903; here Russell speaks of the "Promethean constancy" required of all who would defy a hostile universe. This early "credo" is to be found in the collection of essays by Russell entitled *Mysticism and Logic* (Melbourne: Penguin, 1953), 50–59. [Editor's note.]

parison with the Author of that Plan. Fortunately however, the evidence of Divine Purpose is non-existent. . . . We are therefore spared the necessity for that attitude of impotent hatred which every brave and humane man would otherwise be called upon to adopt towards the Almighty Tyrant.[15]

We may summarize Russell's attitude toward that which is, toward the structure of things, toward what he might call that world of large facts which every person confronts in his nonprofessional capacity, by the statement that if the nature of things is the creation of a transcendent God, then that God is our enemy, and if it is not then the world itself is our enemy, and must be resisted though the fight may be carried on without personal hatred. What man is up against is not something neutral but something that is against him. Hence the proper attitude of man toward the Transcendent is defiance in the name of humane feeling or of spiritual values.

Such defiant utterances of natural religion always call forth strong rejoinders from another tendency in the natural religion of distrust. In the nineteenth and twentieth centuries the answers to Shelley and Russell were of course made in the name of Christianity. But it is highly questionable whether the answers for the most part reflect the reconciliation of man with God in Christ so much as they reflect the natural religion of fear which is only the counterpart of hostility. Express hostility toward cosmic tyranny must be distinguished from that sort of honest questioning of God which occurs in the Book of Job and in 2 Esdras, a questioning which is without fear oppressed by guilt. Similarly the natural religion of fearsomeness is related to the natural religion of hostility as fear is related to courage; both are natural attitudes. But in personal relations they are connected with trust and distrust, with loyalty and disloyalty. The brave man of the Promethean type confronts a distrusted transcendent reality with courage; the brave man trusting stands before God like Job asking for an answer; the fearsome man confronts the distrusted Transcendent with trembling; the fearsome man full of trust is awed but not cowed and there is joy in his awe. In either case, whether aggressiveness or fear prevails, the situation between the distrusted Transcendent and the distrusting self among selves is felt as an antagonism. The natural religion

15. Russell, *Scientific Outlook*, 118, 130f.

of anxiety and fear, however, is either more aware of the all-powerful character of what man confronts than Promethean defiance is, or it is less confident of human power to contend with the "Omnificent," or it is less loyal to fellowmen and simply more self-centered. In any case it seeks to deal with the same situation of enmity between the Ultimate and man which Prometheanism has in view; only its approach is one of appeasement.

Evidences of the religion of fearsome faithlessness, that is, of distrust, so surround us and are to be discovered within the self in such abundance that it is unnecessary to seek for literary expressions. This is natural religion as we know it in history and in contemporary life. We meet it everywhere in early religion, as for instance in the Diasia of Athens which Miss Jane E. Harrison and Sir Gilbert Murray have described.[16] "The Diasia was a ritual of placation, that is, of casting away various elements of pollution or danger and appeasing the unknown wraths of the surrounding darkness. The nearest approach to a god contained in this festival is Meilichios. . . . His name means '*He of appeasement*' and he is nothing else."[17] The subjectivist prejudice of social psychology leads Harrison and Murray to interpret such a figure as the mere projection of the emotion of the ritual.[18] We shall do better, I believe, to think of these shadowy figures, the wraithlike, insubstantial gods of appeasement, as symbols of that Transcendent, that Nature of Things, before which man is afraid. What men have done to appease "the unknown wraths of the surrounding darkness" by means of human and animal sacrifices, by their rituals of placation through burnt offerings and sin-offerings, by physical and mental ablutions, self-castigations, by pilgrimages and prayers, represents a large part of the story of religion in the world. It is not the whole story, but is a large part of the story. If in ancient times the fear of the enemies or of the enemy was expressed in physical actions in which

16. See Jane E. Harrison, *Prolegomena to the Study of Greek Religion* (New York: Meridian, 1955), 11–28; Gilbert Murray, *Five Stages of Greek Religion* (Garden City, N. Y.: Doubleday, 1955), 12–14.

17. Murray, *Five Stages of Greek Religion*, 14.

18. Murray, for example, immediately adds to the foregoing: "[Meilichios] is merely the personified shadow or dream generated by the emotion of the ritual—very much, to take a familiar instance, as Father Christmas is a 'projection' of our Christmas customs" (*Five Stages of Greek Religion*, 14). [Editor's note.]

men turned their hostility against themselves in order that the hostility of the Other might not become active, in later, more spiritual days, their efforts at appeasement have been of a more refined but perhaps not less cruel sort in the self-castigations of conscience. The casebooks of psychiatrists are full of evidences of religious fears appearing in neuroses and psychoses, of poor folk who are filled with feelings of guilt and fear which they explain as due to their commission of sins against God, and every pastor knows how frequently the question is raised, "Did I sin or my parents that this blindness, or this lameness of body or spirit has been visited upon me?" In the natural religion of fear every mischance of existence is explained as an act of vengeance upon the part of the Deity, a hard master who reaps where he has not planted and who requires what he has not given man the ability to perform. The terrors of conscience which haunt the solitude of men are to a large extent the terrors of men who confront an angry Otherness in the world which hunts out every secret fault, not with the love of a Master who undertakes to make his work perfect but with the animosity of a defender of personal glory, the vindictiveness of a finite being who can be deprived of power by other finite beings.

The prevalence and extent of such fear in our natural religion is explained in many different ways. Naturalism undertakes to make a distinction between fear and dread, or between the sort of healthful fear which, aware of definite danger, reacts against it with appropriate animal flight and the sort of fear which has no object. For it the natural religion of fear is a vague fear of the unknown which projects into the world fearful objects—ghosts and wraiths and demons and vindictive deities. Such naturalism believes that as knowledge takes the place of ignorance the fear of the unknown is gradually banished from existence. Existentialism, aware that it is not simply as an animal that man is afraid but as a self suspended in nothingness, regards dread as the concomitant of man's finiteness. Man fears because he not only dies but knows that he must die, because he knows that he is finite. Anxiety is the mode of finite existence and this anxiety expresses itself in man's efforts to find some small security against the surrounding nothingness.

The naturalistic answer does not satisfy because the fear that man entertains and expresses in his fearsome religion is not animal fear; it is not fear of the dangers that assail the flesh. Doubtless it is deeply mixed with this animal fear, but it is a more personal and more social thing. It is the fear of the loss of selfhood, not simply of life; it is the fear of exclusion from the community of selves. It is the fear of death not as a biological but as a personal event. And there is in it always the fear of an other that is devising harm. The Unknown which is feared is not the realm of the as yet undiscovered finite enemies of the body and mind of man, but rather that unknown Fate or Law or nature of things which ordained and will destroy the self. Therefore the ghosts and deities and symbols which to psychologism seem to be projections of an irrational inner fear, may be regarded also as symbols of that transcendent reality which man confronts but from which he flees in distrust. There is an object of this religious fear; what the fearsome man regards as the object is indeed a fiction of his imagination; but the object is nevertheless present. There is something of which he is afraid. It is life itself; it is the principle of life; it is the ultimate reality that he is up against, the counterpart of his existence as a self.

This natural religion of fear is no less an expression of distrust of the Transcendent than is the natural religion of defiance. If defiance says, "I am against God," fear says, "God is against me"; if the former is animated toward defiance by love of its fellowmen, the latter is frightened by the threat of disaster not only to the self but to those whom it loves. It contemplates with horror the implacableness of an enemy who visits the transgression of the fathers on the children and it seeks to avoid by appeasement not only the destruction of the self but of those companions in and with whom it has its existence.

This natural religion of distrust is fortified, and perhaps also rooted in, the social life in which fear of the unknown power is used as an instrument by those responsible for the welfare of the group for the sake of maintaining its solidarity. Through the threats by means of which the social law is sanctioned, men are brought up from infancy with the idea that they are being watched by a vindictive supernatural reality which inflicts punishment here and hereafter on those who infringe upon the laws. The imagery of hell and heaven, particularly of the former, is introduced into the minds in many subtle ways. Over all life there lies the fear of a strange justice which upholds laws that are supernaturally established and unintelligible in rational terms. Life is lived amidst strange taboos; the threat of disaster hangs over it as it touches, tastes and handles the precarious objects of daily life.

Natural religion of distrust of the Transcendent has a third form—
the form of isolation and forgetfulness. If the dark rites of primitive
religion give evidence of the distrust that appears in fear, the bright
and speciously happy converse with the deities of Olympus illustrates
the turning of distrust into the defensive mechanism whereby men try
to forget the presence of the ultimate reality while they construct for
themselves an imaginary world in which they can pretend to be at
peace. In nations facing a political enemy whom they deeply distrust,
not only attitudes of imperialistic, aggressive action and of appeasement manifest themselves, but also of flight into forgetfulness. There
are always those who turn to the pleasures and occupations of the moment, believing somehow that the enemy will disappear if they will
refuse to think about him. Psychiatry offers us illustrations of persons
who when "faced by the cause of dread, [exclude] reality from their
perceptions and [lapse] into pleasurable fantasies." They seek security
from real danger by means of "de-realization (as applied to the outer
world)" and of "de-personalization (as applied to the individual himself)." [19] There is much religion of this sort. It appears in the frequently
lauded bright worship of Greece, but no less in Christendom, perhaps
particularly in spiritualism and in Jesus-pietism, or in a worship of
the Virgin and saints, and of a kind, heavenly Father (insofar as he is
one God among many), which peoples the world the self inhabits with
kindly, beneficent powers, which regards death as an illusion, evil as
mere appearance.

The movement toward isolation may take other forms. It may seek
with Epicureanism to banish the sense of transcendent reality, substi-
tuting for it the multiplicity of blindly running atoms, depersonalizing
the world around as well as the self, dealing with the latter as well as
with the former as a set of atomic moments, separate from each other,
mere events in time and space. The denial of transcendent unity has
its counterpart in the denial of the unity of the self. The flight from
the other is accompanied by the flight from the self while the effort is
made to interpret the world as superficial, without depth or meaning,
without foundation or superstructure. One flees from the ultimate to

19. Oscar Pfister, *Christianity and Fear: A Study in the Psychology and Hygiene
of Religion*, trans. W. H. Johnson (London: George Allen and Unwin, 1948), 42.

the near and tries to live among the things that are close at hand with such peace of mind and such pleasure as one can extract from them.

Whether the effort ever succeeds is questionable. Behind the Olympian deities there always lurked the darker shadows of a Transcendence that needed to be appeased. In mystery cult and in Greek tragedy the evidence is given of the presence of a somber sense of life in the minds of the worshippers of bright Olympian gods. "There is a strange shadow of sadness," writes Gilbert Murray, "hanging over this wise and kindly faith [of Epicureanism], which proceeds from the essential distrust of life that lies at its heart. The best that Epicurus has really to say of the world is that if you are very wise and do not attract its notice . . . it will not hurt you. It is a philosophy not of conquest but of escape."[20] Over it hangs the shadow of the distrusted Transcendent. Of this form of natural religion as of the others it is true, as Kierkegaard points out, that it is an expression of despair, though this despair is the sadder because it is not aware of itself as despair.

WHAT is the source of this deep distrust of that One from which we all proceed? It is a strange fact that the explanations of its presence reduplicate the ideas connected with its various forms of expression. In mythologies and theologies we undertake to account for the fact that our relation as selves to the Transcendent appears in our lives in the perverted form of disappointment. And our explanations seem to follow the three main lines of our effort to deal with the distrusted One. (1) In our defiance we say that we were thus created, thus formed as selves, that anxiety is the natural form of our finite existence. (2) In our fear we blame ourselves, saying that we have fallen by self-will from our original right relation of faith in the Transcendent and that our anxiety is the punishment for our pride in wanting to be independent of the transcendent God or to be like him, living by our own power. (3) In our effort to escape into the imaginary world of the bright gods, into the little cities where we may be faithful to our little loyalties, we say that the whole dread of the Transcendent One is an invention and an illusion, that we have been betrayed into this situation of fear and distrust by untrustworthy fellowmen. In the first case our creation is

20. Murray, *Five Stages of Greek Religion*, 105.

our fall; in the second, we tempt ourselves to our own undoing; in the third, we are the victims of our companions.

From the point of view of a reconciled faith we do not have much interest in asking how and why the fall into distrust occurred, save that with Kierkegaard we rejoice in the idea that before God we have always been in the wrong. Our starting point is not the doctrine of the fall but the knowledge or hope of salvation. Yet there are two points about the fall that are noteworthy: first it is a genuine *fall* and cannot be the absolute beginning of our personal existence; and, second, that it is a complex interpersonal event in which the whole structure of faith is involved.

So far as the first point is concerned, there is wisdom in the saga of the first man and in the theological elaboration of that saga which posits a state of innocence before the fall. If faith is a dimension of personal existence, then it seems clear that distrust or disloyalty cannot be the first fact. Distrust is only possible where the conditions for trust have first been established. One cannot suspect another of lying and deceiving except in a situation where loyalty is expected. A promise must be made before it can be broken. The negative relations of distrust, disloyalty and disbelief all presuppose the previous establishment of trust, loyalty and belieffulness. Lies are an impossibility in a world where there is no truth, whereas the opposite is not true. Faithlessness does not eliminate the order of faith but perverts it. The order still exists; if it did not, not even distrust would be possible. If "fall" means distrust of God and disloyalty to Him it cannot mean the total destruction of our relation to God; it must rather mean that an ambivalence has entered into our personal relations which poisons and corrupts them. Hence distrust cannot be the fundamental element in our relations as selves to selves, above all to the Transcendent.

In the second place, since the structure of our faith is so complex it seems evident that the perversion of the relationship which is involved cannot easily be blamed in a mechanical or an individualistic manner on an isolated act or person. Is the first act of faithlessness distrust or disloyalty? Is it disloyalty to God or to companions? Is it an act of disloyalty toward the self by a companion or by the self toward him? In our distrust we seek to place the blame. It is, we say, the woman who tempts the man with her distrust; it is the serpent who distrusts

God; it is the giving of a commandment, the demand for loyalty, to one who is unable to bear the responsibility, which is responsible for the great debacle. But the fall of man precisely because it is an event in the faith relations of persons is an event in which no mechanical relations of cause and effect are present. Here disloyalty and distrust, self and neighbor, are so involved that the distrust of God is a response to the companion's deception or disloyalty and the self's disloyalty in the breaking of its own promise is another source of its distrust. For Luther the first sin is distrust which tempts man to break the law or his promise. But this distrust in God, this belief that he will not keep his promises, presupposes a desire or a will to break faith, since one does not suspect another of promise breaking if one has had no experience of it in oneself. When we look at the disorder of faith, at distrust and disloyalty in their manifold interrelations from the point of view of reconciliation, then the effort to place the blame on one criminal, whether the self or companion, whether the ancestor or the contemporary, evaporates in the recognition that all have sinned and that this does not mean that each one has sinned by himself but that all have sinned together.

This sin is personal; it is the sin of the self in interpersonal relations, but it is not individual. There is no way of carving an individual self out of the web of responsible relations and setting it before the bar of justice as alone responsible. Before God it is man who finds himself in the wrong, but not man as distinguished from fellowmen. In the history of our faithlessness every man is his own Adam but no Adam is alone in his sinfulness; none falls in solitude. His solitude is a consequence of fallenness, not the cause of it. This is not to say that the fall of man into distrust is a social event over which the individual has no control. It is an interpersonal event which is something quite different from the sort of social event we encounter in our institutions. In an interpersonal event every person participates with loyalty and disloyalty, trust and distrust; but none is in it alone and no decisions are purely individual decisions. Each act calls forth the moral reaction of others and is itself a reaction to the anticipated or remembered moral action of companions.

The story of each personal life makes clear how interpersonal the fall is. The self comes to awareness of itself, of its companions and of the common life with a sense of promise. The "promises of God" to us do not designate certain statements which are said to have been made to Abraham and his children. They designate that sense of meaningfulness and splendor with which personal being awakes to existence. There is in the background of existence, whether as memory of childhood, or as Platonic recollection of something heard in another existence, or as the echo of an inner voice, the sense of something glorious, splendid, clean and joyous for which this being and all being is intended. It is not a selfish or individualistic sense of promise, as though one felt oneself preferred to others or as though the promise would not be kept unless others were granted a smaller share of everlasting vitality. That mean and narrow mode of thinking comes later. The promise of life is the promise of glory and splendor, not for me, but for existence and for me as a part of this world of being. But to our personal life which begins with such a sense of promised brightness there comes, whether in childhood or adolescence or later, the great disillusionment. Things are not what they seem. The great tragic note which runs through all human literature and philosophy— the distance between appearance and reality—is sounded. Behind the splendor of life there is the putrescence of death. The virtues of our families and our friends cover deep shamefulness. There is a shame within ourselves. We also are not what we seem. Behind the pleasure and the kindness about us there is wretchedness and cruelty. The odor of death, the feeling of betrayal, the sense of pollution, invades all our existence. That things are not what they seem and that what they are is infinitely sadder, darker and more disappointing than what they appear to be—this is the theme which runs through Greek and modern tragedy, through Eastern and Western philosophy. Eastern thought speaks of Maya, the illusion, and Western thought contrasts with the daylight view of a natural world of sound and color the night-view of a scientific world in which there is neither music nor artistry appealing to the eye. Through the pages of our literature move the Oedipuses and Hamlets, deceived in those they love and in themselves. Physical nature, society and they themselves are full of the great illusion. To Hamlet

> this goodly frame, the earth, seems . . .
> a sterile promontory; this most excellent canopy,

the air, look you, this brave o'erhanging firmament,
this majestical roof, fretted with golden fire,
why, it appears no other thing to me but a foul and
pestilent congregation of vapors. (II, ii)

while of himself he says:

I am very proud, revengeful, ambitious; with
more offenses at my beck than I have thought to
put them in, imagination to give them shape, or
time to act them in. What should such fellows as
I do crawling between heaven and earth? We are
arrant knaves, all. (III, i)[21]

What shall we say of the sources of this great sense of deception
so common among men? Who is the betrayer? Where was the first
promise broken? The self, beginning with the sense of promise, with
acceptance of its security and a stable world, of the loyalty of its parents and companions and with assurance of its own integrity, awakes
to a deception that is in it and all around it. Things are not what
they seem and what they are seems always worse than the appearance. It learns to live in the midst of distrust and in the expectation of
disloyalty.

This state of fallen faith is historic and human as well as personal
and immediate. When we contemplate our human history, this net-
work of interpersonal relations, it is not difficult to describe it as the
history of treason. When one reads the story of the nations and notes
how broken treaties and deceitful promises mark each page, one wonders why anyone at any time should accept another promise, write
another treaty. There is no area of human conduct—not economics,
not religion, not the family—which is free from the wreckage of broken words. The massive law books and the great machinery of justice
give evidence of the vast extent of fraud, deceit and disloyalty among
men. Treason begets distrust, distrust treason. In the great fear that
all life is a deception these selves who cannot live except by faith seek
to gain a little satisfaction by new faithlessness. In the knowledge that

21. See Theodore Spencer, *Shakespeare and the Nature of Man* (New York:
Macmillan, 1942), 94ff.

they must die, that the promise of life is a deception, they seek to maintain themselves a little while by making promises they do not intend to keep and by pretending to trust where they are deeply suspicious.

But all this life of man among broken words and deceitful promises remains a life of negative faith. It cannot be lived on the level of animal fears and stratagems. For it is the perversion of the life of faith. It cannot be lived as though loyalty and trust were not the required and actual conditions of existence. It cannot be lived as though there were no selves living by loyalty but only by instinctive actions moving toward the attainment of desire. The great disorder of our existence cannot be eliminated by a return to the innocence of a life in which there is no promise and no loyalty and therefore neither treason nor deceit. We are fated to be loyal and to live by trust but all our loyalty appears only in the corrupted form of broken promises, and our trust in the perverse form of the great suspicion that we are being deceived.

6

THE RECONSTRUCTION OF FAITH[1]

Our human dilemma is this: we live as selves by faith but our faith is perverted and we with it. Without acknowledgment in trust of other persons who have bound themselves to us in loyalty and without a covenanting binding of ourselves to them as well as to causes that unite us, we do not exist as selves; we cannot think, we cannot communicate with objects or with one another. Without interpersonal relationship in faith, in the great triadic interaction of self, companions and cause, we might perceive the data offered to our senses but it is questionable whether we would possess concepts. Without interpersonal existence of which faith—as exercised in the reciprocities of believing, trusting, and being loyal—is the bond, there might indeed be experience from given moment to given moment but the continuity of the self in its experience would be hard to define, if indeed such continuity would be thinkable. But now all this personal-interpersonal existence is warped, twisted and corrupted, so that our believing is accompanied by disbelieving, our trust is accompanied by distrust, our loyalty by disloyalty. We acknowledge one another as persons but in distrust —as persons who cannot be counted upon to be faithful though we ought, being persons, to keep faith. So we are forever on our guard, not against error but against the lie; we suffer less from ignorance than from deception. Being finite, unable to penetrate very far into the unknown, does not cause us anxiety so much as being subject to illusion. So we raise the question ultimately whether all our reputed

1. In the handwritten Stone Lecture, "Jesus Christ and the Reconstruction of Faith," HRN wrote in the top margin the following alternatives for *reconstruction*, all of which he crossed out: rebirth, regeneration, reformation, revival, resurrection, renovation. See notes 2 and 3 below. [Editor's note.]

knowledge is not a grand myth, invented by no individual person but the product of our interpersonal interaction. Is not our science itself a great construct, a useful invention, a practical device? At the heart of this problem of deception and distrust is our relation to the nameless, ultimate Transcendent and Circumambient. The human distrust of life, of reality, of that out of which all things come, may in part be a result of all the deceptions and betrayals to which men have been subject in their relations to fellowmen, but to an even greater extent it seems that the temptations to deception and betrayal of companion by companion arise out of the distrust of Being. Because we think that if we do not maintain ourselves we will not be maintained; because we believe that if we do not fill a fleeting existence with values we have ourselves put there it will become valueless; because we deeply doubt that the Being or the source of being will bring success to our causes; therefore we think we cannot afford to keep our promises to each other, separately or in groups. The chain of distrust and disloyalty grows in length and complexity. The interpersonal interaction weaves back and forth with deceptions that call forth distrust, with distrust tempting to new betrayals, with families, nations and religions participating in the great confusion of the life of faith. This is our anxiety, a result not of our finiteness but of our dependence on an infinite and on finites which have the freedom to deceive us.

There is no escape from the dilemma. We try to escape by means of universal skepticism, saying that we will believe no one except ourselves and nothing but what is evident to our own reason and senses; that we will accept no promises in the social realm but confine ourselves to obedience to pure power; that we will count upon no pleasures except those offered us in each moment. But there is no escape; for we cannot live to ourselves even in our individual reason and sense experience, which often deceive us or in which we deceive ourselves when we do not seek and receive the validation of our companion reasoners and coexperiencers. Experience is unformed and inchoate as purely private experience. Formed by reason it is formed by ideas that are no longer private but socially known. The effort to escape from the perversions of faith in society by accepting nothing but power is equally frustrated, since pure unified power does not exist among our fellowmen and if, by obedience to one power, I give promise of supporting it against its adversaries I have again involved myself in responsibility for keeping faith and have opened up the possibilities of being deceived. Nor can I escape from the dilemma of counting upon the fulfillment of life's promises while also living in fear of disappointment, by confining myself to the pleasures of the moment. I cannot escape because I live as a self with a future; my present pleasures have consequences which I anticipate. I cannot escape because not only my greatest pleasures but all of them have a social character, so that even the food I eat and enjoy comes to me salted and seasoned with the love and hate and the sense of duty of my fellowmen.

There is no escape from life in faith and no escape from an existence in which all trust and faithfulness is malformed by distrust and treason.

Though there is no escape from life in faith, so disordered, into life without faith, there is a prospect of salvation from diseased faith. There is a prospect that this vast and complex disease in interpersonal existence will be healed. More than that, there is the assurance that a new promise, namely the promise of healing, will be kept. This is the prospect and this is the promise of which Christians speak. This is the New Covenant, which is not a substitute for the old promise given with life but is based upon it, yet so that it is not only the reinforcement of what we once believed but the answer to our disbelief of the first promise.

There are, to be sure, two ways in which we can reflect and communicate as Christians. We may do so as members of the rather amorphous society which is called the Christian religion or we may do so as those for whom the primary companion in all thinking and interpretation is Jesus Christ. In the one instance we seem to abstract again from the life of persons in interpersonal relations and hence from life in faith; we think and speak as subjects who deal with objects, who recommend to others that they hold certain beliefs, who espouse a certain ethics. In this situation we speak of Christian faith as consisting of a certain set of beliefs urged upon us by the Scriptures, or by the church or by Jesus Christ himself. We contend for the validity of these beliefs against those of our companions who are skeptical either of the astuteness or of the honesty of the writers of the Scriptures, of the theologians of the church. In turn we question either the wisdom or the integrity of those fellowmen who question the existence of God, the historicity of Jesus, the efficacy of the sacraments, or the value of

Christian virtues. But when we try to communicate as such members of the Christian society we cannot be wholly objective. In this life in the churches we are concerned not only with the ceaseless effort of men to communicate with each other about their common world and themselves; we are also deeply involved in the whole complex disease of our personal relations; these churches are the objects of distrust on the part of members of other societies, religious and secular, who deeply suspect them of desiring to gain power rather than trust them to keep faith by speaking truth honestly as they see it. They are accused and in part they confess that they have not only broken their promises to men and nations but have also betrayed the cause for the sake of which they say they exist. Having promised by their acceptance of Jesus Christ as their Lord to love one another as he loved his disciples they have from the beginning fostered hostility toward certain companions; having obligated themselves not to shun crucifixion and death, they have denied their cause whenever they have been threatened with extinction, adapting themselves to the needs of the time; having accepted discipleship to the poor man they are very anxious about food, drink and clothing. There is no need to recount at length the various features of the churches' disordered life of faith. Nothing is more evident in human history than the fact that the church as the historical society of Christians had its origin in Judas' betrayal and Peter's denial quite as much as in Jesus' faith and that it tries to continue in existence by means of repeated acts of faithlessness to its cause and to its companions.

Yet inside and outside these churches, partly in dependence upon them, more largely as that which sustains them even in their faithlessness, there is another Christianity. It is not an affair of organizations, of doctrines, of beliefs, of rites. Neither is it an ethics in the ordinary sense. Neither is it individual piety. It is rather the interpersonal movement of faith that centers in the person of Jesus Christ; yet it does so in such a way that he directs all trust and loyalty away from himself to the Transcendent and Circumambient. This is the hidden movement in the churches and in men: this is the life which comes to appearance and yet is at the same time hidden in the prayers of men who have come to acknowledge Christ; it is manifest and disguised in their personal encounters with the Transcendent. In this interpersonal life Jesus Christ is not the founder of a religion; he is not an object about whom

believed and disbelieved doctrines are taught, as when his two natures
are defined, or his place in the Trinity is examined. He is personally
present as Master and Lord. He is the personal companion who by
his loyalty to the self and by his trust in the Transcendent One *reconstructs* the broken interpersonal life of faith.[2] He is not only present
as a mystical alter ego—the Christ who lives in the Christian so that
the Christian no longer lives without Christ. Jesus Christ is present
in the interpersonal relations not as memory or as spirit dwelling in
each one as an isolated unit, but as the center of a community of persons present in history. As such, not as the founder of a religion, but
as person among persons he carries on a work of salvation "by faith
unto faith," the work of making us whole in our faith relations. It is
with Christ in this existential sense as the one who is directly present
in our life in faith, not as one about whom we hold certain beliefs on
the authority of a church or a Scriptures which we more or less distrust, that we are here concerned when we raise the question about our
human dilemma of faith. When we say this we do not mean that there
are some human beings who are members of a church and others who
are personal members of the interpersonal community of faith. What
we mean rather is this, that at the level of our existence where we are
personal Jesus Christ is not an object, but a person. He is trusted and
receives loyalty; he is not an object of our teaching, not the object of
a common knowledge, but the acknowledged companion.

WHEN we reflect on the life of faith in and with Jesus Christ as the
companion of the trusting and would-be loyal self, we find that what
is present is not a Jesus of history but the Christ of faith, not Jesus
incarnate, but the risen Lord. The given fact is not some historical
truths which the self believes on the basis of its confidence in other
persons, such as apostles and gospel writers, though such truths are
also believed. The given fact is Jesus Christ as the present companion
of the persons who trust him and seek to be loyal to him. When we
speak of faith in Jesus Christ we speak of the fact that we pray in his
name to the Father, that we inquire into his mind and seek with him in
interpersonal community to understand our present world, our fellow-

2. Emphasis added. *Reconstructs* has a quite specific meaning here and throughout. See note 3, below. [Editor's note.]

men, our duty and our future. The beginning for us is not historical or
theological and conceptual but a present personal beginning. We cannot begin with "creation" when we begin in faith and ask, "How can
we move forward from creation to incarnation, from incarnation to
crucifixion, from crucifixion to resurrection, from resurrection to the
session at the right hand of power?" Neither can we begin with certain
historical facts, then move on to the witnessing and recording of the
facts. When we attempt to do this, either in the fashion of speculative
or of historical theology we try to move from the not-self to the self,
from neutrality to faith, from the past into the present. We are trying
to move then from the unknown to the known, from what we do not
believe in, from that to which we have no personal relation, to the immediate and the believed. In reflection upon ourselves as believing and
unbelieving persons we can only begin with what is given and move
on from there forward and backward. We cannot proceed from a preexistent Christ to an incarnate Christ, we can only move backward
from the contemporary Christ to the historical, from the historical to
the preexistent.[3]

3. See George Herbert Mead, *The Philosophy of the Present*, ed. A. E. Murphy
(Chicago: Open Court, 1932). HRN simply refers to Mead's work without elabo-
rating on its relevance to his own inquiry. But the procedure he is following here
is in general conformity with the analysis Mead presents in "The Present as the
Locus of Reality." Mead rejects the notion of an "in-itself" past. Such a past could
appear only in some world that transcends our experience. We "reconstruct" the
past from the vantage of the present. Hence, we do not move in a simple linear
manner from the past to the present but rather also from the newly emergent
present to the past. "My original proposition," Mead writes, is "that a reality
that transcends the present [viz., the past] must exhibit itself in the present" (11).
Again: "The picture which this offers is that of presents sliding into each other,
each with a past which is referable to itself, each past taking up into itself those
back of it, and in some degree *reconstructing* them from its own standpoint. The
moment that we take these earlier presents as existences apart from the presentation of them as pasts they cease to have meaning to us and lose any value they may
have in interpreting our own present and determining our futures" (9; emphasis
added). It is reasonable to suppose that the author's choice of the word *reconstruction* for the title of this chapter, from among the many possibilities he wrote
in the top margin of the first page of the Stone Lectures version of this chapter, is
partly due to the special significance with which Mead endowed the term. HRN's

The Jesus Christ we acknowledge in personal trust and loyalty— slight as it is—is Jesus Christ risen from the dead, Jesus Christ among us. He is to be sure a Jesus Christ who is among us as remembered. In similar fashion we never acknowledge another person present to us except also as one who is remembered. If I count upon a person to aid me I do so as one whom I recognize, remember. He is the same person as the one who has been in my past. To be introduced to a man is not to recognize him as a person. When I acknowledge him in trust and distrust I do so as one who remembers something about him, rightly or wrongly. So we remember Jesus Christ in our very coexistence with him.

Moving backward from the present givenness of the Jesus Christ in whom we trust and to whom we want to be loyal we remember him as the one who was introduced into our personal-interpersonal existence by persons who trusted him, were loyal to him, with him were loyal to us and our companions, trusted with him in the Ground of Being and had God for a Father, by persons who were trusted by us. He was not introduced into our personal-interpersonal lives by objective historical scholars who, examining the records of the past, discovered more or less authentic documents of the life of a human subject who made certain interesting statements about God and man and the times in which he lived. But if we were introduced by them to him as a person, it was not by their scholarship, but by their faith-relation to him and to us. We become acquainted with him and his character in the interpersonal family of those who are his companions and whose companion he is in trust and loyalty. As we move backward and forward we find that this is always the situation. There is no possibility of gaining access to Jesus Christ except as he is presented to men by those who have faith in him. All men who encounter Christ did so first of all in the loyalty to him of parents, benefactors and friends. The fact that these benefactors or friends are often also officials of the religious institution called the church has not been of first importance. They commended themselves as persons to trust by their integrity and their loyalty to the selves to whom they communicated Christ; the

line of argument appears to be, then, that the *present* Jesus Christ of faith is the companion who reconstructs the faith by which we have lived in the past. [Editor's note.]

commendation was not attached to ordination. For reliance upon an institution never brings forth personal trust and loyalty, though the accumulation of personal trust in representatives of an institution does foster dependence upon that institution. Moreover when the approach to Jesus Christ was made sooner or later through the Scriptures the situation was not changed, for once more he was presented only as the acknowledged counterpart of the subjective faith of those who believe in him. If by the Jesus of history we mean an individual as he appeared to men who saw him but did not trust him, who heard him but were not moved to be loyal to him and his cause, who witnessed his words and deeds but were not brought to rejoice in their sonship to God, then it is apparent that if such an individual existed he no longer exists. This so-called Jesus of history left no mark upon physical objects as Cheops or Pericles or Hammurabi did which all men can see so that they can conclude: "There was a great builder here at some past time." He founded no empire which can be regarded as his enduring creation and the manifold marks of whose presence can lead us to deduce the existence of the founder. Even if we regard the visible church as such an empire the evidence that Jesus founded this complex institution is not convincing, since there is no rite or teaching of that church the origin of which we cannot assign to some author other than a Jesus of history. There are so many traces of so many architects. He left no writings which we can read with critical examination of his style and for the purpose of tracing out what was original with him, what was climate of opinion in his time, what was an echo of the books he read. The words and phrases ascribed to him come down to us in a language which he did not speak and those of them which are not the evident inventions of other men—such as his speeches in the Fourth Gospel— can be ascribed to other rabbis of the time in which he is said to have lived. Thus skepticism about the trustworthiness of those who have given reports about Jesus can flourish. And any confidence in him as savior based on confidence in those who reported his deeds, whether scripturally or in the church, is a tenuous thing.

But now though a Jesus of history, knowable as an object among other objects or as a subject among other thinking, perceiving, desiring subjects is inaccessible to us, there can be no question that the Jesus Christ of faith is a fact, and an unconquerable fact in our history. This Christ of faith does not wait for us to discover him as we must try to discover those historical beings who have left the traces of their erstwhile biological existence on the landscape and institutions. We encounter him. He meets us. And he meets us in the persons we encounter. He does not meet us as he met Paul on the road—a flash of light and a disembodied voice—and yet there is something like this in our meeting. For we do not meet him incarnate but as risen. He meets us as the unseen head of a company of believers in him, that is, of men and women who seek to be loyal to him, for whom he is the cause, who trust him. It would be foolish to say that these are persons who believe the writers of Scriptures and assent to their statements that Jesus Christ was born during the reign of Caesar Augustus and perished when Pontius Pilate was procurator in Judea. Of course they believe these statements and many more besides, but their trust is not in the writers of Scriptures and their loyalty is not to holy words. Their faith is not the belief that once upon a time Jesus Christ existed. Their faith is in Jesus Christ and they treasure Scriptures because they tell of Christ, not vice versa. Jesus Christ as the Christ of faith is the focusing point of a company of believers. He meets us, we meet him, not as perceived but as one to whom the eyes of others are directed, not as an idea in our minds but as a person who accompanies in unseen presence those who believe in him, who are loyal to him and who trust him. This company of believers is made up to a large extent of men and women who are no longer objects of our perceptions as human beings in the flesh. They are nameless in part, such as those writers of the gospels and the general epistles, who are undoubtedly historical figures who have left traces of their physical existence in their handiwork. In part they have names, being such persons as Paul and Francis and Bernard and Luther and Pascal and Wesley and Kiekegaard, Edwards, F. D. Maurice and Horace Bushnell. In part the company consists of those now living. But the company is present to us even without perceivable representatives. When we have the Scriptures in our hand we are in the presence of the company of these believers in the Christ of faith, persons of trust and loyalty. The Christ we see is the Christ reflected in their existence, the Christ who is hidden and yet pointed to in their devotion, the savior who is suggested but not revealed as they pray "Abba, our Father."

Since we have been so often deceived, since the massive propaganda for causes in which men believe has so often led us to accept as real what later we discovered to be partly fiction, since our distrust of life is so deep that the promises connected with this Christ seem too good to be true, therefore our skepticism now asserts itself in the reflection that such a figure as this Christ is a myth. He has all the characteristics of a mythological figure: he is present only in reflection, in the attitudes of men who believe in him; he is the symbol of their unity; he is the dramatic representative of what they want to believe; he is the anthropomorphic image of a cause. Yet he differs from all other mythological figures we know, for these are personifications of general ideas or rites or of laws of nature or of communities. They are Persephones or Agnis or John Bulls or Athenes or Brihaspatis.[4] But if the Jesus Christ of faith is the personification of anything it is of the idea of personality itself, of the principle of faithfulness. And what these believers in him present to us is not an idea, described so that we can recognize it as we conceive it ourselves, but by their acknowledgment of trust in him they present a person, one upon whose loyalty to his cause and theirs and to them they count. It remains possible that this Christ of faith is a mythological figure in the sense that he is the personification of the idea of faithfulness, of self-binding and consistent loyalty, a personification generated continuously in the minds of believers in him, a "docetic" Jesus Christ. But as acknowledged person, as individual relied upon and reliable in his freedom he is then also an historic figure, a being strange in his discarnate power to compel the faith of incarnate companions.[5]

We may attempt to say this in another way. The Christ of faith, the focusing point of that company of persons who in their faith in him invite us by their loyalty to us and to him, is a living Christ. The ques-

4. Persephone, daughter of Zeus and Demeter, stolen by Hades and made his queen of the lower world but allowed to return to earth for six or eight months of each year. Agni, the fire god of Vedic Hinduism. Athene, the patron goddess of Athens. Brihaspatis or Brhaspati, the chaplain and sacrificer for the gods in Vedic Hinduism; god of wisdom and poetry in post-Vedic literature. [Editor's note.]
5. In his discussion of the social character of the present G. H. Mead argues that a "present object" may belong to two different systems simultaneously. We cannot reproduce his subtle analysis here, but Mead's entire essay is directly relevant to the large issue at this point in HRN's text: Jesus Christ may belong both to a "myth system" and to the historic past. See chapter 2, "The Social Nature of the Present," in *The Philosophy of the Present*. [Editor's note.]

tion about this Christ is not "Did he arise from the dead?" but "Did he ever die?" It is not "Does he exist?" For his existence in power is manifest in the faith of those who are bound by loyalty to him, who live in trust and loyalty to the one to whom he is loyal and who invite our trust and loyalty. The questions we are raising are rather "Did he at one time exist also in another form as a subject known by other subjects and in a body perceptible to other perceiving bodies?" and "Is his existence as a person dependent upon the personal faith of other persons?" To these questions there cannot be a final answer based upon a confidence in the absolute truthfulness of eyewitnesses, for "What eye," we ask in our skepticism, "cannot be deceived?" Nor can we answer on the ground of absolute trust in the possibility of an objective existence apart from all subjective relations to it. Docetism is always a possibility to our skepticism, to that large remnant of unbelief in us which asks whether our creator did not create us to be deceived by our senses and by our subjectivity. But even to docetic Christians so far as they are not thinkers only but persons Jesus Christ is person and even these docetic Christians introduce into our lives by their loyalty and devotion, not by their skepticism, the person of Jesus Christ.

It remains true Jesus Christ is in our personal history as the focusing point of persons who have faith in him and who by faith in him come to be men of faith. The Jesus of our history is the Christ of faith.

T H E Christ of faith, that is, the Christ who has been introduced into our personal histories by the faith of those who trust him and are loyal to him in his loyalty, is a specific individual figure. We meet him in the company of those who believe in him: not as an empty point on which their eyes are focused in trust and faithfulness, not as an indefinable companion, but as a specific figure; he is one with whom, because of whom they say "Father" to the Incomprehensible Transcendent One. They *communicate* Jesus Christ to us not as an idea but as a living and dying human being. The communication may seem in the first place to consist of recollections of those who were eyewitnesses, percipients of certain data given to the senses.

They saw, or claimed they saw those who had seen, a certain man called Jesus of Nazareth who wandered about Galilee and Judea attended by a devoted band of followers, performing marvelous cures of the sick, raising the dead. They heard from him, or claimed they heard from those who had heard him, about God and human life, as well as certain predictions about his own fate and other coming events including the destruction of Jerusalem and the end of man's life on earth. But we are not dealing after all with recollections and recollections of recollections. We are dealing with Jesus Christ as a specific figure in the lives of those who believe in him. We do not confront a recollection of Jesus Christ mediated to Paul by the twelve, but Jesus Christ reflected in the faith of Paul. And this Jesus Christ is not a remembered figure but a living being present with his past to Paul. He is communicated in this manner to us not so that we remember certain stories about Jesus Christ who once lived but so that Jesus Christ, as this specific figure with a specific past, is born again in our minds. Not ideas about him are communicated but he is communicated. The process has a certain parallel in the realm of ideas. We may say that what happens to us in communication is that we are reminded of certain ideas which we have always known but need to recollect in Socratic fashion, as when the idea of unity in multiplicity is the subject of discourse. But we may also say that the idea of such unity is generated in us in the midst of communication. We now have a direct relation to it, not via the communicator. Something like this happens in the case of Jesus Christ—the specific individual with his past is generated in us. He is communicated so that there is no longer absolute dependence on the communicator, though in this case as in all others our personal relation to the reality is never a lonely one, without companions.

The striking feature of this Jesus Christ of our history is his faith and the striking feature of his fate is his betrayal. His faith has the three aspects which we have discovered in analyzing the structure of faith in interpersonal relations, with this marked difference that the cause to which he is loyal is the rule of the absolutely Transcendent One. His faith is first of all the faith of trust in the Lord of heaven and earth who had thrown him into existence in such a manner that he could be the object of Joseph's and his people's distrust. His trust is in this Lord of heaven and earth as One who has bound himself to care for the apparently most despised beings, human and animal and vegetable in his creation. He trusts in the loyalty of the Transcendent One and in his power, being certain in his mind that nothing can separate men from the love of God. He trusts God for himself, for his nation, for mankind, for animals. This trust is wholly personal. He has the assurance that God will never forsake him, that he is the dearly be-loved Son, that he is the heir of God. With this completeness of trust in God as wholly loyal, without the least deceptiveness in his nature, the Jesus Christ of our history combines complete loyalty to men. He is without defensiveness before them for he is certain that God will defend him. He does not trust his fellowmen but he is wholly faith-ful to them, even or perhaps particularly when he chastises them for their disloyalty to each other and their distrust of God. He seeks and saves the lost. He spends himself for others—and always with trust in God. As person, as living in faith, this Jesus Christ is Son of God. To try to explain this miraculous sonship to God physically, as some early disciples did in stories of virgin birth, seems to add nothing to its remarkable character. It is the personal relation of a faithful, trusting, loyal soul to the source of its being which is the astonishing thing. This is a superhuman thing according to all our experience of humanity. Yet it is humanity in idea, in essence. This, we say, as we regard him, is what we might be if we were not the victims and the perpetrators of treason and distrust.

It is, therefore, never difficult for men to believe that the Jesus Christ of faith existed once upon a time in natural, biological form. This per-sonal miracle of the existence of a man of complete faith, of universal trust and loyalty, is conceivable. He is conceivable as the abnormal possibility of our normal human existence in negative faith. We do not doubt our fellowmen when they tell us of the loyalty of Jesus Christ. We are not inclined to believe that they are deceiving us. What we doubt is not the possibility of such goodness; but we are skeptical of its power—not of the miracle of goodness, for we somehow see that the appearance of such loyalty and trust is not in contradiction of the laws of personal existence. It is rarely suggested that the goodness of Jesus Christ is mythological invention.

Now, further, the Jesus Christ of faith whom we remember was the subject of betrayal. His trust in God was profoundly distrusted as an attitude dangerous to the existence of his nation, of its cause as the people of God, of its leaders, its worship, its laws. This confidence in the loyalty of God is suspected as something which is demonic. This loyalty to all men—Samaritans and Romans, as well as Jews, to sin-ners as well as righteous, to the despised as well as the esteemed—is seen as dangerous to all treasured values. He is distrusted in his trust in God and in his loyalty to God and to God's creatures. Again we discover that the story of Jesus Christ's betrayal is easy to accept. Our experience of human existence is such that we are quite ready to agree that given such faith, such distrust and betrayal of it would be a natural outcome among men. "This," we say to ourselves, "is the way it had to happen, as the prophets had foreseen. Given such a servant of God what other outcome would be possible under human conditions?" The specific historic conditions are secondary. Had Alexander ruled instead of Caesar, had the leaders of the Jewish people been kings instead of priests, had the people been Greeks instead of Jews, had the son of God been named Socrates rather than Jesus, still when a servant of God came, this surely would have happened, he would have been profoundly distrusted because of his trust, because of his loyalty to God, and because of his loyalty to all the creatures of God. The predictions of the prophets, especially of 2 Isaiah, represent simply a profound understanding of the nature of human distrust and disloyalty, an understanding based on faith in God and the experience of centuries of faithlessness.

If ever there was an opportunity in human history for the reconstruction of faith, for the self-disclosure of the Incomprehensible Transcendent Source of being as God, as wholly loyal to his creation, as redeemer of all the promises given with the gift of existence itself, then it was at this point where faith in him became incarnate. But the faith of Jesus Christ came to the end of its historic existence with the cry: "My God, my God, why hast thou forsaken me?" There was faith in the cry: "My God!" But it is the uttermost cry of faith, at the edge of nothingness. If at this point in the central tragedy in our history there had occurred the demonstration of the power and glory of the God in whom he trusted; if Elijah had come; if he who saved others had been saved; if we know not what natural or supernatural event had taken place to deliver this soul of faith from death and further shame; then might not faith as universal loyalty and universal trust have been reconstructed among men?

This did not happen. In our distrust we should not expect it to have happened. Should the Son of God come again, it would not happen. But something else has happened; something that is very ordinary and very strange, something over which we wonder. In consequence of the coming of this Jesus Christ to us we are able to say in the midst of our vast distrust, our betraying and being betrayed, our certainty of death and our temptations to curse our birth: "Abba, our Father." And this we say to the Ground of Being, to the mystery out of which we come, to the power over our life and death. "Our Father, who art in heaven, hallowed be thy name" (Matt. 6:9–12; Luke 11:2–4). "I believe, help thou mine unbelief" (Mark 9:24).

I T seems most strange that by that recollection which we have of the betrayal and the disastrous end of the one who trusted in the Power of Being as utterly faithful to him, we should have had introduced into our lives a little ability to trust. It seems most strange that when the one who had heard and believed the promise of life given to him —"Thou art my beloved Son"—that when this one had the promise of life canceled—that then we should in the recollection of this one believe that his God is indeed our Father, that his Father is the De-terminer of our Destiny. This is the resurrection of Christ which we experience. In and through his betrayal, denial and forsakenness, we are given the assurance that God keeps his promises. In and through and despite this we hear him, we read him, we accept him as God's word to us that God is faithful and true, that he does not desire the death of the sinner, that he is leading his kingdom to victory over all evil, that we shall not die but live, that the last word to us is not death without ending, but life everlasting.

We cannot penetrate far into the miracle of resurrection as this mira-cle takes place in the interpersonal life of faith. But we can discern a few aspects of this historical, ever-repeated event. First we can under-stand that in order that the Jesus Christ of faith should not have been distrusted, rejected and betrayed, it would have been necessary for us human beings to be wholly different from what we are. If all our his-tory from the beginning of our remembered common life had been different, then, of course, this event would also have been different. If all men had kept faith with each other from the first act of free loyalty onwards, and if men in their freedom had always trusted God as the sparrows trust him in their lack of freedom, then Jesus Christ might have been welcomed as the perfecter of faith, its universalizer and guarantor. But history without sin, without murder, treason, lie, is not our history.

Second we can understand the consequences to our faith if the faith-

ful Christ had been saved from the consequences of human distrust
and betrayal by the sort of miraculous interference he himself knew to
be possible: the twelve legions of angels of whom he spoke, who might
have been Roman soldiers arriving in a nick of time to save Pilate from
fear of insurrection, or who might have come in the form of a natural catastrophe which would have upset all the plans of princes and
priests, or who for that matter might have arrived as superterrestial
beings—men from Mars. Jesus Christ might have been spirited away
after the fashion of Elijah and saved from death. What would the consequences for our human faith have been? Just about nothing, so far as
we can see. We should doubtless say, if he was remembered at all, "We
do not know what happened to him" or perhaps, "He was an unusual
person and was translated into another existence, but as for us, we
must all die. He was loyal; but we are disloyal. He trusted; we must
distrust. How could we be delivered, even to the slightest degree, from
our disloyalty to one another and to God and from our distrust of him
by an event which merely showed that there had been one exception
to the rule that all men must die?" The consequence might well have
been a greater concentration than ever on our desperate effort to avoid
personal death no matter what happens to others. It might have been
a stronger belief than ever that God is a hard taskmaster demanding
the uttermost from us in order that the rare reward might be given.
For most of us the despair would have been heightened.

But it is what happened that is important for us, not what might
have happened. What has happened is that this forsaken and rejected
Servant of God has been given a name above every name among us.
What has happened is that he has entered into the life of the human
world as the most persistent of rulers, the most inescapable of companions. His eyes are still upon us when we deny him; he is forever
warning us about our ambitions to be great; he is always here teaching us to pray. He is built into the structure of our conscience, not so
that we cannot offend against him, but so that it is he who is offended
in our offenses. He is present with his wounds and in his rejection in
all the companions whom in our great disloyalty we make the victims
of our distrust of God and our diseased loyalties. That Jesus Christ is
risen from the dead and that he sits at the right hand of God exercising power over us, that is one of the most patent facts in interpersonal

history. Our evidence for it is not in beliefs about empty tombs or about appearances to others, but in our acknowledgment of his power. C. H. Dodd has pointed out that among early Christians there were evidently men who, like the writer of 1 John, did not move forward from an experience of Christ rising from death to the Christ seated at the right hand of power, but backward from their acknowledgment of the latter to the conclusion that therefore he had risen from the dead.[6] This doubtless is the manner of much personal conviction in our time, for we live in the time of Paul and not in that of Peter and the twelve.

In our relation to this betrayed, forsaken, destroyed and powerful Jesus Christ we are enabled to qualify our distrust of the Ground of Being so that we pray to the mystery out of which we come and to which we return, "Our Father who art in heaven." Jesus Christ, we say, reveals God. What we can mean by that does not seem to be what certain theologians seem to think, that apart from Jesus Christ we do not acknowledge God at all, for we do acknowledge him with perhaps all of our human companions in the distrust manifest in fear, hostility and evasion; yet we do not acknowledge him as God, as the supreme object of our devotion, as the faithful one in whom we trust, as the one in whose kingdom we are bound to loyalty to all our fellow citizens in creation. There is an acknowledgment even of the personal element in the Ultimate in this distrust and anxiety of ours. But it is perverted faith. What appears to happen in fellowship with Jesus Christ to our life of faith is that our distrust of God is turned somewhat in the direction of trust, that our hostility is turned slightly in the direction of a desire to be loyal, that our view of the society to which we are bound in loyalty begins to enlarge. The thunderclouds on the horizon of our existence are broken; the light begins to shine through. A great metanoia, a revolution of the personal life, begins in us and in human interpersonal history.

We explain what has happened to the life of faith, in which just and unjust live, by saying that in this coming of Jesus Christ to us the Son reveals the Father and the Father reveals the Son. The Son reveals himself as Son in his moral, personal character. By his trust in the

6. See C. H. Dodd, *The Johannine Epistles* (London: Hodder and Stoughton, 1946), xxxiii. [Editor's note.]

Transcendent Source of Being, by his loyalty to all to whom he trusts the Father to be loyal, by his faithfulness to God he makes himself known to us as one who has the character of a Son. Hence he is recognized widely as the good man, the man who is son and brother. But he is not made known as Son of God in reality until he is established in power, until it becomes clear that such a character of trust and loyalty is indeed in complete harmony with the nature of things. By his resurrection from the dead, by his establishment as ruler of life, by the power of his resurrection as Paul has it, it is established that the Transcendent One is indeed what Jesus Christ in his faithfulness and trust acknowledged him to be, and it is equally established that the faithful servant is acknowledged by Reality itself. The Father reveals himself as Father in the resurrection of the Son; the Son is revealed as Son by his life and his resurrection. In both instances much was known of the creator and of Jesus Christ prior to the revelation to faith of the Father and the Son. It was known and acknowledged in distrust that there is an Absolute; it was recognized and acknowledged in distrust and suspicion that Jesus Christ regarded himself and acted as though he were a son and as though the Ultimate was his Father. What happens in the establishment of Jesus Christ in power over our personal life is that the double hypothesis of his historical existence is validated: The Lord of heaven and earth is indeed the faithful, loyal Father, and Jesus Christ is indeed of one nature, one faithfulness, with that Father.

We may describe what happens to faith by saying that the two great problems of existence are solved at least in principle. The first of these is the problem of the goodness of Power. The great anxiety of life, the great distrust, appears in the doubt that the Power whence all things come, the Power which has thrown the self and its companions into existence, is not good. The question is always before us, Is Power good? Is it good to and for what it has brought into being? Is it good with the goodness of integrity? Is it good as adorable and delightful? On the other hand we know something of what true goodness is. We recognize goodness in every form of loyalty and love. But our second great problem is whether goodness is powerful, whether it is not forever defeated in actual existence by loveless, thoughtless power. The resurrection of Jesus Christ from the dead, the establishment of Jesus Christ in power, is at one and the same time the demonstration of the power of goodness and the goodness of power. But the demonstration remains a demonstration of a God who is both Father and Son, not of a Father who is identical with the Son or of a Son identical with the Father. When Jesus Christ is made known as Lord it is to the glory of God the Father. And the Absolute is made known as Father in his glorification of the Son.

7

THE COMMUNITY OF FAITH

Our reflections on faith, if they have been correct to any degree, open up to us the prospect of further reflective inquiries, of the formulation of hypotheses on various subjects, to be tested by reflection; they raise questions about the relations of these findings to other findings by theologians who have made some other aspect of the life with God, with Christ and our companions the object of their reflection, such aspects for instance as love and hope and wisdom and dependence. Were the task of the theologian that of a systematic philosopher then he would be required to build upon the foundations he has laid a complete structure of propositions relating to all the parts of the Christian life. But if the primary task of theology is not that of building a total and coherent system of reflections but rather that of understanding and clarifying as much as possible a given set of data, then theology must in all honesty refrain from the effort to build a system and content itself with the effort to discover the relations between various parts of the given reality.[1] Specifically, such theology will understand that neither faith nor love, neither wisdom nor dependence, is the foundation on which the Christian life rests; that the foundation is God, Father, Son and Holy Spirit; and that the unity which is present in life with God and Christ and neighbor comes from Him and from Him

1. See above, chapter 2, "The Method of Reflection." See also the author's brief discussion of the task of theology in chapter 1 of *Radical Monotheism and Western Culture* (New York: Harper and Brothers, 1960). Notes accompanying the handwritten manuscript indicate that when HRN suggests that the "primary task of theology is not that of building a total and coherent system," among his contemporaries he had Barth and Tillich principally in mind. But see note 2 below. [Editor's note.]

alone.[2] But this divine foundation no man can lay. To seek to base the life with God and one's companions on anything less than Him—even though this be faith, or love, or hope, is to fall into the temptation of idolatry. We cannot inquire or speak from God's point of view, not even in a theology of the word of God.

OUR attention is drawn to these limitations by the impossibility of developing an adequate understanding of the reality and the work of the Holy Spirit on the basis of such a theory of faith as has been set forth above. There is no need when we speak of faith as acknowledgment of and trust in the reality of faithful, self-binding, promise-making and promise-keeping selfhood to develop the binitarian formula, so prevalent in Christianity, into a Trinitarian formula.

We are, to be sure, dealing with spiritual principles, that is, with internal elements in man and God, when we deal with faith. God, the Creator, we say in our reflection on faith in him, is a being who binds himself, who makes and keeps covenant. The Creator has this spiritual character and we cannot speak of him otherwise than in these spiritual, personal terms. It is wholly inadequate to describe him as absolute Power. He is absolute Person. To act in faith is to address him personally as "Our Father," to trust him as Being which is free with the sort of freedom we know not in nature with its forces acting externally nor in mind with its capacity for attention but in personal relations, where self binds itself to self. There are those theologians who, analyzing some other aspect of the life with God, find it difficult to ascribe personality to the Ground of Existence, but the fact that personality or spirit in this sense does not come into view when we inquire into our feelings of absolute dependence or into the ideas which meet us in the depths of reason does not entitle anyone to say that personal categories are more symbolic than are categories of power or of idea. Faith, trust in the fidelity of the Creator, is acknowledgment of him as personal, directly expressed in prayer and in commitment, indirectly expressed in the proposition that God is spirit, in the sense of personal spirit. Man trusting and seeking to be faithful is aware that infinitely much more must be said about the Creator; that many symbols must

2. Perhaps Schleiermacher ran into his greatest difficulties and errors in trying to build a system of theology on the basis of the idea of absolute dependence.

be employed in communication about him; but such communication cannot dispense with the personal symbol which refers to something in reality that cannot be otherwise referred to and which is acknowledged as directly present where the fundamental act of personal faith is enacted in the prayer: "Our Father." The analysis of faith leads then directly to this conclusion, that the Creator is Spirit, in this sense of "spirit," that he is Being with the inner reality of selfhood, covenanting and keeping faith.[3]

Again the analysis of faith gives us the understanding that there is something in the inner life of man which has been implanted there by the Creator. Man is a living soul, not only as one in whom there is breath, or in whom there is experience and thought, but as one who cannot live except as he lives by faith. He lives as a self, a deformed and sick self to be sure, yet as self who binds himself before he breaks the bonds, who trusts before he distrusts and is faithful before he can be faithless. There is a spirit in man, which not only proceeds from the Father in the sense that man was and is being so created as to be and to become a covenanting self, but also in the sense that this inner selfhood is in every moment dependent upon the presence of that Other Spirit, a Universal Thou.[4]

In the third place the analysis of faith makes clear that the Lord Jesus Christ is spirit, so that in Pauline terms this theology of faith must affirm "The Lord is the Spirit" (2 Cor. 3:17). The Christ of our life in faith is not simply the historic individual Jesus, though he is that too, but he is the inner personal companion who as person is present in the memory and expectation of the believer. He is acknowledged as person. The Christians who can say, "It is no longer I that live but Christ who lives in me" (Gal. 2:20), may be few and far between, but those Christians are numerous who can make the second part of the statement in some such form as this: "Christ is the personal com-

---

3. Related handwritten notes show that it is Paul Tillich's position on the unsuitability of the language of personal being with which the author is chiefly disagreeing, though of course Schleiermacher also invites similar criticism. [Editor's note.]

4. In place of the words "that Other Spirit, a Universal Thou" the author had originally written: "that polar Spirit from which it derives its being at the same time that it proceeds toward it." [Editor's note.]

panion who has been engrafted into my personal existence so that I
cannot and do not live except in this companionship. I am untrue to
him, I deny him, but he does not let me go and I cannot let him go."
This Lord is Spirit also in the personal sense; he is a being who has
and does bind himself to us in our community as the constant companion. He is a being on whom we rely in trust, though we trust him
for different gifts than those we expect from the Father. The unity of
this Spirit of faith, which is Jesus Christ in man, with the Spirit of
the Father and the Spirit which proceeds from the Father is not one
of identity, according to the analysis of faith, though the inner life of
spiritual selfhood in community is a unified life. Personality precludes
identity.

When we have said this we have said that the third principle in the
Deity of which our beliefs speak does not appear from the point of
view of the analysis of faith to be a person as the Father and the Son
are persons. The three persons who are involved in the community of
faith are Father, Son and this poor human self which has by creation
and redemption been lifted into the unbelievable privilege of commu-
nion with Father and Son and with all those other persons into whom
God has breathed his Spirit. *Spirit,* rather than being a third personal
principle in the Deity, is an attribute of the two persons in the Godhead and that which makes it possible for us to be selves with them.
We are thus led to a kind of binitarian formula; God is Father and
Son in two persons. The Spirit is that which, being of the very nature
of God, is given and matured and restored to human persons. It is the
principle of community among selves who are united in trust and loyalty to Father and to Son. But Spirit on the basis of this analysis is not
person in the sense in which Father and Son are.

We could argue for the general correctness of this position on two
grounds. First, we could call to mind the prevalence of the binitarian rather than of the Trinitarian formula in the Scriptures and in the
church.[5] Second, we could attend to the direct language of faith in

5. At this point the author refers to A. E. J. Rawlinson without specifying further what in Rawlinson's work he is alluding to. In *The New Testament Doctrine
of Christ: The Bampton Lectures for 1926* (London: Longmans, Green, 1926)
Rawlinson discusses at some length the relationship between Christ and the Spirit
in the writings of Paul and of the Fourth Evangelist. With respect to the former

prayer and in oaths of loyalty. We offer our prayers *to* the Father in the name of the Son, in the words of the Son, with the Son as our companion.[6] We pray, to be sure in the Spirit, but this Spirit which makes it possible for us to pray is not another person besides Father and Son; hence we rarely address him in prayer; though occasionally devotion prays, "Come, Holy Spirit," more frequently it prays to the Father for the gift of the Spirit.[7] The language of loyalty does not differ much from the language of trust. Loyalty directs itself primarily to Jesus Christ and secondly to his cause—"his sake"—which is the Father and his cause. It follows Christ, binds itself to Christ and with him binds itself to the universal cause of the Father. It is not "natural" or usual for Christian faith to commit itself in allegiance to the Holy Spirit. The Spirit whereby we are enabled to make our vows to Christ and to his cause is not a person or cause to which we make our vows.

But we are stopped from developing these reflections to the point where they become positive assertions to the effect that the idea of personhood is incorrectly applied to the Spirit or that the binitarianism of Christian faith-expression should take precedence over the Trinitarianism of Christian belief. From the point of view of an analysis of faith, as from the point of view of an analysis of love, Trinitarian belief may indeed seem speculative, but we are inclined to regard all beliefs to be speculative which are founded on analyses we have not ourselves made. The theological statements of members of our community about the Holy Spirit may rest not at all upon speculations but upon genuine inquiries into realities of the spiritual life of man with God which we

---

Rawlinson writes: "If S. Paul's language is not always explicitly Trinitarian—and it would be absurd to expect to find in his writings a technical statement of the doctrine of the Trinity—his theology is nevertheless in a general sense Trinitarian in tendency . . . , he has given classical expression to precisely those elements in the Christian experience of God which were in the long run to render a Trinitarian theology inevitable" (159). HRN evidently was as much if not more interested in the textual evidence Rawlinson brought forward than in his conclusions. [Editor's note.]

6. There is a monarchian element in all our faith.

7. For example, the much used collect from the Sarum Rite begins with "Almighty God, unto whom all hearts are open," continues with the petition, "Cleanse the thoughts of our hearts by the inspiration of thy Holy Spirit," and concludes with "through Christ our Lord. Amen." [Editor's note.]

have not made ourselves. They may rest upon real communications of God with man of which we are not so aware as we are of faith and love. That this is true in the case of the doctrine of the Holy Spirit appears on all the pages of the New Testament which testify to the experience of spiritual power quite different from that with which we are familiar. Moreover all the Christian mystics in all times speak to us of an experience of the Holy Spirit which again is not the normal experience of a great number of Christians.

In this situation we may take one of three attitudes. First we may say that that which we do not experience and which we have not been able to experience does not exist, that Pentecost is legend, and spiritual healing an error of interpretation since all that is present is faith healing, that experiences of spiritual power and mystic vision are psychological, not theological phenomena. We may, with an Emil Brunner, set the word in opposition to mysticism and declare spiritualism in ancient and modern forms an abnormal or heretical manifestation of faith, while we declare our own theologies of faith, or love, or hope or the word to be normative not only for us but for all Christians.[8] Second, we may make trust in our Scriptures and in our church our point of departure and believe all that they tell us without seeking to reenact for ourselves under their guidance the experiences of which they speak and without seeking to understand what has become a part of our own existence. Trusting the Scriptures and the church we shall then believe that there is a God, that he is Father, Son and Holy Spirit. In that case not our encounter with the Ground of Being and with the Christ of our personal history is normative, but the past encounters of other members of the community is the norm. In the third place, however, we may refrain from making either our existential experience and our

8. In his polemical book on Friedrich Schleiermacher, *Die Mystik und das Wort* (Tübingen: J. C. B. Mohr, 1924, 2d rev. ed., 1928), Emil Brunner censures mysticism as being antithetical to faith in the Word. He plays Goethe's much quoted lines, "Feeling is everything / Name is sound and smoke," against Luther's "Verbum est principium primum," and writes that whoever (in this case Schleiermacher) renounces "Name," content-determined faith, whoever renounces faith, whose content is word, surrenders to mysticism; the necessary result is the reduction of *spirit* to *thing*. "Either mysticism or the word" (2d rev. ed., 88). Here, as elsewhere in the margins of his copy, HRN registered his skepticism of Brunner's argument. [Editor's note.]

understanding of it or the records of the experiences of the founders of our community normative. We shall consider only one reality as normative, God in Christ, Christ in God, to whom the faith of the past and ours is directed and from whom it proceeds. And in this situation we shall not be afraid to speak of what we know, but neither shall we be without reverence for what other men have known, though we no longer know it or do not yet know it. We shall not repeat the beliefs of the past as statements reflecting our own faith; this we cannot do and still keep faith with our fellowmen; yet we shall trust these men of our community who so reported what they understood of their life with God and we shall think of these beliefs as reports and as prophecies. Sometime, perhaps, we shall understand the reality to which they refer. This applies to many of us when we deal with the beliefs about the Holy Spirit. We also say that in our life in faith we know that God is Spirit, that the Lord is Spirit, that the spirit in the human being proceeds from the Father and the Son, that the Spirit which proceeds from the Father and the Son is interpersonal reality. We can attach great significance to the statement that the Spirit is consubstantial with Father and Son. What we cannot say for ourselves is that the Spirit is not the Father, that he is not the Son, and that he is equal to Father and Son —as a power or a person like them but distinct from them. But those of us who speak in this fashion are not in a position to deny that the classic formulation is true. We can believe it; it is not an expression of our trust in God, however, and not an oath of loyalty to him but only an expression of our lower trust, our secondary but real loyalty to the community of faith which has so expressed its trust in God and so made its vow of fidelity. I believe that there is a Holy Spirit.

BECAUSE of this situation in which we believe as assenting to the statements of a community in which we have confidence and because of the question which arose at the end of the last chapter concerning the results of the restoration of faith by Jesus Christ, we are led to the final part of our analysis of the structure and history of faith as the interaction of personal trust and loyalty in the triadic community. What is the history and extent of the community of faith as restored by Jesus Christ and what is its relation to the visible religious societies and institutions which we call the Christian church or churches or Christian religion?

Faith, as we have seen, is not something which exists in a person. It is an interpersonal relation; nor does it exist simply between two persons save insofar as they have a cause which transcends them. The community of faith which rises into view as the great possibility with the restoration of faith in the Creator by Jesus Christ is the community of every self with God and all God's creatures. It is the community of selves who trust God in his loyalty to all that he has made, to all the companions of the self; it is the community of fidelity in which all selves bind themselves and are faithful to all their companions as those to whom God is faithful. It is the community in which Christ is the companion in every company, for which not a sparrow falls from the roof top without participation in the death and resurrection of Christ and in which what we seek to do in loyalty to our companion Christ is done in loyalty to the least of his brethren. In the company of the faithful God is the cause of all and God's cause is their cause. Faith as loyalty moves from the creation to God who is creation's cause, since it is there to glorify him, and it moves from God to his cause, which is the creation that he loves and redeems. The community of faith which dawns upon our view through the restoration of faith by Jesus Christ is the kingdom of ends of which Immanuel Kant and Albrecht Ritschl spoke; in which every one is an end to all other selves, no one a mere means; but it is more; it is the brotherhood of man in fidelity and trust of which the Social Gospel spoke; it is the glory and the sovereignty of God of which John Calvin spoke; it is the restoration of that groaning and travailing nature which is waiting for the adoption of the sons of God of which Paul and Origen spoke. It is a universal community of faith grounded in God and existing toward him as well as in mutual relations. This is the possibility; rather it is the promise which rises into view with the restoration of trust in the Ground of all Being as faithful to all that proceeds from him. It is the community of infinite interactions of loyalty, in which there is never a doubt of the center of faithfulness, from and to whom all trust and fidelity proceed, but in which there is no doubt either that loyalty to him means loyalty to all his creatures, respect for man, but not only for man; reverence for "life," but not only life, loyalty to being, to all that is God, and he is all in all.

This community of faith rises into view as something both given to our present and promised to our future, as something which has

been and is being established by the faithfulness of God and as something which calls for the willing, devoted, strenuous exercise of human
fidelity. Since faith is not only trust but trust in loyalty and cannot trust
in God's loyalty to our companions without itself being challenged to
loyalty to them, the community of faith is necessarily human work in
response to the divine. The will to believe is involved in the restoration
of faith.[9] What Jesus Christ does in the restoration of faith is not only
to reconcile us to God so that we can trust in him, but to challenge by
his fidelity to God and to God's cause, the creation, the response of our
loyalty. In some Christian reflection, notably Luther's, the greatness of
the gift of trust in God was so magnified that all human response of
loyalty to him and the neighbors was represented as almost automatic
consequence of trusting faith. But a person, as a responsive being, is
not a machine. Where through the restoration of trust all the conditions have been established for fidelity, there still fidelity is called for as
an act of personal self-binding, of commitment. The dreadful freedom
with which we are created as persons who can be traitors or who can
be loyal is not taken from us by the restoration of trust in God through
the fidelity of Christ. Now just because some trust has been established the challenge to commit ourselves, to maintain our integrity in
loyalty to universal Being in the universal kingdom is issued with a
new force. The restoration of trust is in this fashion a most vigorous
challenge to the will to believe, that is, to the will to be faithful to the
universal cause and to all our companions in it, whether we feel like
it or not, in sickness, health, prosperity, adversity. It is the challenge
to be faithful in all relations to all companions since God makes them
his cause in all their relations. Trust in God knows that his kingdom
of faithfulness will come. Trust in him as wholly loyal not only to us
but to all our companions knows that he will not allow a kingdom
to come which is not established in the faithfulness, the willing, free
devotion of all its members. Hence in faith we have the bittersweet
assurance that all our sins are being and will be forgiven, which means

9. Although the author does not here or below set off *the will to believe* in quo-
tation marks, "The Will to Believe" as well as "The Sentiment of Rationality"
are well marked in his own copy of William James's essays, *Selected Papers on
Philosophy by William James*, ed. C. M. Bakewell (London: J. M. Dent and Sons,
Everyman's Library, 1918). [Editor's note.]

for us that through our suffering and the vicarious suffering of our companions every treason will have to be made good. The restoration of faith is the challenge to a life of continuing responsibility. By faith we are called to the work of faith; through trust we are challenged to will to believe, to will to be faithful, to will that every treacherous flaw in us be made right. Trust is gift; God's loyalty to us and to our companions is sheer grace. The response of loyalty to Him and them in Him is our task and our responsibility.

Because this is so the promised perfection of the community of faith is both a longed for and a feared consummation. It is longed for as the realization of all that is potential in our creation and redemption, as the deliverance from all deceits, lies, treasons, hypocrisies which distort our existence. But it is also feared as that which brings to light and eradicates all that is false in it. The prayer, "Forgive us our sins," is something like the petition we address to a surgeon: "Cut out my cancer." The prayer, "Thy kingdom come," is something like the petition addressed to a powerful empire: "Put down our rebellion." The prospect of faith's full restoration includes not only the prospect of infinite effort, but of great suffering. Yet if these fears cause "perturbations" of faith, as John Calvin called them, the gift of trust and of the will to be healed are ever renewed and are stronger than fear. In another sense the promised restoration of the community of faith causes perturbation and anxiety in the midst of confidence and trust. Since it is faith, trust and loyalty in interpersonal relations which is in question, there always arises into view as the counterpart of the community of faith the possibility of treason. There is progress in personal relations of faith; trust experiencing loyalty increases: loyalty calls forth loyalty. But such loyalty is accompanied by the dark shadow of treason. The more extensive the community of loyalty, the more extensive in its effects will be the act of treason which breaks that loyalty. The more men trust in one another's loyalty the greater the temptations to the abuse of that loyalty, the greater also the temptation to deceit or to hypocrisy. Great vices are possible only where there are great virtues, since vice always feeds on virtue. Hence the possibility of the anti-Christ always appears in the future of the community of faith, while its progress is marked by the appearance of deceits and treasons that are the counterparts of its faith. There is therefore always this threat in our future and this sin in our present in the restored community of faith, though in that restoration faith is certain of this one thing, that treason can never be the last word, that faith is always the victory which overcomes the world. Nevertheless the prospect which opens to faith is never one of painless progress, but a prospect of arduous struggle, of suffering and betrayal, ending in the victory of the one who does not will the death of the sinner, but that he shall turn from his ways and live.

If the community of faith which rises into view with Christ's act of restoration is eschatological and teleological in this fashion, it is no less historical and archaic, as having been with us from our beginnings. The statement "I believe in the Holy Catholic Church" is a personal statement of trust and loyalty which we make in the context of our prayer and oath of allegiance to the Father and the Son. As a forward looking statement it is a repetition of the statement, "I trust in God, the Creator and Savior," for it is an affirmation that we trust the Creator of the whole for the whole. This is his cause. Because we trust in him and in Jesus Christ therefore we look forward to the establishment of the whole creation in the unity of a Holy Assembly of faith. It is also an oath of allegiance, an act of commitment to universal loyalty, to keeping faith with all men in all relations of life. But the statement looks backward as well as forward. We live our personal-interpersonal lives in memory and in hope. As a backward-looking statement it is one of trust as well as of loyalty. "I believe in the Holy Catholic Church," as an utterance of faith, is an acknowledgment of the presence to us of the community of faith which stretches backward as the long procession of those who trusted and were not put to shame, who were loyal to their companions in their loyalty to the God who kept covenant with them all and were hallowed as he required their covenant keeping with each other. The community of faith is not divided into the living and the dead. For those who are divided from us by time are not more remote than those who are separated from us by space. There is no greater distance between the faithful in the nineteenth century and those in the twentieth than between those who live in America and those who live in Asia. But the temporal relations in which we live as persons are different from those which obtain between our physical and biological existences. They are different too from those which prevail as mind has converse with mind across the centuries of natural time. Our relations to men of faith who lived in the sixteenth century are not mediated by all the men who have lived between these times biologically. There is a kind of foretaste of the resurrection of the dead in the community of faith. We find ourselves standing alongside Luther and Calvin and Pascal as they and we confront the same transcendent, mysterious Creator, and are reconciled by the same Lord Jesus Christ. Where the same God is present to us there is a presence of us to each other. The contemporaneity we experience in our perceptive life, when we find ourselves confronting the same object—such as the sun in a certain position in the heavens—is an analogue to that contemporaneity of the life we live in faith, when we find those who are dead yet speaking to us, because they are in the same situation personally in which we are. The church of the past is a present church, not to perception but in our life of trust and loyalty.

If we say that the church of the past is present to faith we may be misunderstood to be saying that it is merely "believed" to be present.[10] But faith as personal existence in trust and fidelity does not "believe" what it does not see—that is a negative statement.[11] It *acknowledges* that which it trusts and to which it is loyal.[12] It is in this sense we "believe" in the community of faith which belongs to all ages of the past: we trust it in its trust in God and in its loyalty to all companions. We encounter God and Christ directly but in this company, and we acknowledge him God and Lord not by ourselves but in this company. We do not first trust in this church and then in God; the relations are direct but double. We trust in God as we have been led to understand the mysterious One by the church. The dialogue has always been a double one and is now a double one.

In that community of faith which we trust as loyal to God, loyal to men, loyal to us, there are no distinctions. There is here no Jew nor

---

10. *Believed* is evidently here being used in the sense briefly discussed in chapter 2, "Believing and Knowing," as the holding of a conviction that is at least "objectively insufficient." [Editor's note.]

11. The allusion here is to the episode of Thomas doubting the report of the other disciples that the risen Christ had appeared to them, in John 20:25. "Unless I see . . . I will not believe"; and verse 29, "Blessed are those who have not seen and yet believe." [Editor's note.]

12. Emphasis added. *Acknowledge* has here the sense ascribed to acknowledgment in chapter 3, pages 40ff. [Editor's note.]

Greek. There are no B.C. and A.D. companies. The faith of Abraham is as great as the faith of Paul, the trust of the prophets is as great a gift, their loyalty as much to be relied upon as the faith of the apostles. It is a very catholic church, this community of faith to which we are related in memory and in personal trust. As the Hebrews who beginning with a covenant established through Moses looked backward and saw that a covenant between God and men as well as among men had been established through Abraham and prior to that through Noah, and prior to that through sinful Cain and fallen Eve, so we looking back from the covenant established through Jesus Christ see that it is the renewal, the confirmation, the elaboration and the partial fulfillment of the covenant made by God with man from the foundation of the earth and witnessed to by seed-time and harvest, by rainbow and by social covenants, in marriage, in political constitutions, in the community of truth-seekers. It will always seem dangerous to our thought bound by the categories of sun-time and earth-time and wanting to think only of a progress forward, not of one backward in this natural world, thus to speak of the Holy Catholic Church in which we believe as one which includes Jews and Greeks as well as Christians. But faith must confess that the trust and loyalty restored by Jesus Christ puts us into personal relationship with all those who expected the redemption of God, with all who relied upon his faithfulness.

This community of faith speaks to us preeminently through the voice of the Holy Scriptures. When we deal with the church as the community of faith and the Scriptures we are not dealing with two different companions of ours in the life of faith but with one. For what are the Scriptures except the confession of trust in God and loyalty to him and the report of what happened to those who believed in him and were not put to shame? What are they but the interpretation of the words of God given directly to generations of men? They speak of what these men of faith have heard and seen, what their hands have handled of the word of life. They give us their prayers and confessions of sin. They are the present incarnation of generations of the community of faith. They are not writings about religious experience of the numinous, though reflections on such experiences are also found there; they are not intellectual reflections on the Ground of Being, though such thoughts also appear in them. They are preeminently the Scriptures of faith. They are the report of the dialogue of divine faithfulness with human distrust and trust. They are the reflections of the Promise of God, of the word that God has given, and of man's acceptance, rejection and reenactment of that promise. They are the books of the Covenant. The Promise of God does not come to us through them, it is made directly to created man, but the community of faith through this record, through this report of its acceptance of the divine promise, interprets for us the encounter in which we stand directly. Jesus Christ does not come to us through the Scriptures; he presents himself to us in the whole community of faith as the risen Lord; but without this testimony of the Scriptures all our interpretation of who this is whom we encounter would be confused and full of error. The Word of God, God's address to us, calling us to repentance and to faith in him, does not come through the Scriptures, but directly in all the encounters of our life with immovable reality, but how should we understand these words or know who it is who is speaking did we not have the interpreter at our side, the community of faith represented by the Scriptures, speaking to us through them?

There is a Protestant doctrine of Scriptures which is the counterpart of the Roman doctrine of the church and of the Deistic doctrine of nature. It places the Scriptures between God and the selves who are addressed by him. The idea is hierarchical. God speaks to the church, to nature, to Scriptures, these in turn speak to us reporting what God has said. This view seems fallacious. A mediator who establishes our trust in God must stand alongside of us as our companion before Him, not between us. So long as my trust is in the church and I believe what it tells me about God, so long I distrust him as one who has not accepted me as his child. Mediation is companionate and neighborly, not hierarchical and aristocratic. The Scriptures are the indispensable handbook, the indispensable companion, the interpreting community of faith at my side in all my encounters with God, with Christ, with my neighbors.

If Scriptures and church are one and the same principle, the community of faith at our side, interpreting the word of God, presenting the living Christ of faith, the chief question which arises is that of the canon. For any specific individual person the canon of Scriptures which have authority, interpreting and in this sense revealing authority, will differ from that of other persons. The canon of sacred Scriptures will differ from period to period in his life. The same thing is true of groups of Christians. As in the second century the canon differed somewhat from place to place, so in the modern world. There can be little doubt that the Westminster Confession has been actually more powerful as interpreter of God's words and acts than the Book of Proverbs for many Presbyterian Christians. Luther's Catechism, the Book of Common Prayer, the Heidelberg Catechism, Pascal's *Pensées*, Augustine's *Confessions* have often exercised greater influence in the community of faith as testimonies of faith than have Leviticus and Jude.[13] We are dealing here not with arbitrary selection but with the fact that God in his faithfulness provides us with companions who interpret his word for us. Some of these companions are so representative of the community of faith that they are rarely without power, such as the Psalms, the Gospels and Paul's letters. They always seem to speak to faith out of faith. They are established by no human decision. They have been put into our history by a process of selection in the community of faith which is at least as irreversible as the process whereby Plato's *Dialogues* and Kant's *Critiques* have been selected and established in the community of thought. They are simply acknowledged, received and consulted with gratitude. They are gifts of God through the community of faith. Others are less established. If we now accept as canon of sacred writings a list narrower and broader than that which functions for us individually and in groups as the indispensable interpreting representatives of the community of faith this is because we seek to realize roughly but as best we can in our visible church the structure of the invisible but known and real community of faith.

Thus we come to our final problem. When we say "I believe in the Holy Catholic Church" we speak of our trust and loyalty to the interpersonal community past, present and future of those who trust in God and in that trust swear and keep faith with him and all his creatures. It is the community of those who keep promises in a universal sense and acknowledge their betrayals as universal betrayals. That this community of faith is not identical with the visible societies, institutions, actions, rites and organizations we also call by the same name of church is very evident. The difference is not the one to which

13. It seems likely that the author had in mind Luther's Large Catechism. [Editor's note.]

Augustine referred and which the Reformers reasserted, namely that the visible church is a mixed body containing faithless as well as faithful persons. We cannot, particularly when we see how interpersonal faith is and how much a person exists by trust and loyalty, distribute faith and faithlessness by individuals. Every person, so far as he is a self, participates in the life of faith and is a subject of redemption, thus belonging to the Catholic church more or less actively. Every person, so far as he participates in the anxiety, distrust and disloyalty of the world—that is to say every person—is outside the community of faith. The line between church and world runs through every soul, not between souls. Neither is the distinction between visible and invisible church as idealism makes it, that is between the actual and the ideal church, a tenable one. For the church in which we believe, on which we count as the supporting, interpreting community of faith, is actual, interpersonal reality, not a form, but an action, trust and loyalty experienced over and over again.

How shall we distinguish between the church we trust and to which our loyalty under God is given and the church in which we worship, whose creeds we recite, whose educational programs we carry forward, to which we speak and sometimes in our speaking preach the gospel? That they are not identical appears from the fact that the Scriptures of the community of faith have not come out of this organization, though decisions about the canon do. But the men of faith who speak in the Scriptures are often not recognized members of the visible organization. As prophets they are mostly unofficial, nonordained, irregular, amateur spokesmen for the visible church. Jesus himself is rejected by it. Paul establishes his credentials with difficulty. The visible church gives fictitious names to the writers of the Gospels in order to make them regular. The visible church establishes its distinctions from the community of faith by the anxiety of its life, by its fear of death, by its compromises with lies, by its efforts to induce men to put their confidence in it or in its rites, or in its Bible.

It is forever involved in the great inversion whereby man turns back upon himself and his works, back upon his faith, away from the God of faith. When it seeks to correct this tendency in one direction, as when it reacts against the idolatrism of subjective reliance on religious feeling, it swings into the opposite direction and substitutes right doctrine about God for God himself. History and contemporary visible church life make it quite clear to us that when we say "I believe in the Holy Catholic Church" we cannot mean this church. And yet, without it the community of faith does not exist, anymore than the personal self which lives by faith exists without mind and without body.[14]

14. The manuscript ends with the following paragraph, which points forward to some of the subject matter the author discusses in *Radical Monotheism and Western Culture* (1960). "One may venture certain speculations. So one may carry forward the hypothesis that the visible church consists of our religious life in society, partly transformed by the faith of Jesus Christ, just as the family, partly transformed by that faith is a Christian family, and the nation, insofar as transformed by Christ is a Christian nation. It is then the natural religious life of man becoming Christian religion, and takes its place in the total history of mankind alongside Christian philosophy and science, Christian economics, Christian politics. Insofar as our religion is the central element in our existence its reconstruction is of central importance as its fall has the most disastrous consequences. But the reconstruction of faith is not something confined to the worship, the numinous feelings, the relations to the unseen world. It is something that extends into the whole of life. And so we see how the community of faith not only comes into appearance in our religious life, where it modifies, transforms, corrects our constant tendencies to fear, but in our domestic and our total cultural life." [Editor's note.]

TABLE OF MANUSCRIPTS

A list of principal unpublished manuscript materials by H. Richard Niebuhr relating to *Faith on Earth* appears below. The list does not, however, include every unpublished piece on the subject of faith written by the author.

1. "Knowledge of Faith" (four chapters, typed)
    1. "Faith Seeks Understanding"
    2. "Towards Understanding Understanding"
    3. "Faith Is a Relation between Selves"
    4. "The Trialectic of Faith"

A letter inserted in this folder, from the editor to the author in the academic year 1946–47, concerning the first two chapters, indicates the tentative title assigned to the manuscript and the approximate time of composition.

2. "The Nature of Faith" (four lectures, typed and handwritten)
    1. Variously titled "Questions of Faith" and "Faith in Question"
    2. Variously titled "The Triple Bond," "Faith Is a Relation between Selves," and "The Threefold Bond"
    3. "The Community of Faith"
    4. Variously titled "The Mediators of Faith" and "The Mediation of Faith"

These lectures were delivered at Lancaster Theological Seminary as the Swander Lectures in November 1950.

3. "Knowledge of Faith" (five lectures)
    1. "Knowing and Believing" (typed)
    2. "The Structure of Faith" (typed)
    3. "The Broken Structure of Faith" (typed)
    4. "Jesus Christ and the Reconstruction of Faith" (handwritten)
    5. "The Community of Faith" (handwritten)

The author delivered the above as the Stone Lectures at Princeton Theological Seminary in the academic year 1951–52. Apparently no record exists of the month in which he gave them.

4. "On Faith" (six chapters, typed and with hand revisions)
   1. "Faith in Question"
   2. "Believing and Knowing in Community"
   3. "The Structure of Faith"
   4. "Broken Faith"
   5. "The Reconstruction of Faith"
   6. "The Community of Faith"

The manuscript is undated. With the exception of the first, the chapters are variously numbered and indicate that one chapter has been removed by the author. On chapter 3, "The Structure of Faith," the author has penciled in, "Omit the first section." See item 5 below.

4a. "Chapter I—Faith in Question" (typed, with hand revisions)
This item is annotated "Draft" and dated "Summer 1952."

4b. "The Knowledge of Faith," "Chapter One: Faith in Question" (typed, with hand revisions)
This item is annotated "Revised Aug. 1953" and is typed on a different machine from that used for item 4a.

4c. "Faith on Earth: An Inquiry into the Structure of Human Faith," "Chapter One: Faith in Question" (typed, with hand revisions)
The general title is handwritten above the typed and crossed out title "The Knowledge of Faith." It incorporates still more revisions than item 4b above. Hence, it evidently postdates the 1953 revision. On page 2 the manuscript bears a penciled reference to Michael Polanyi's *Personal Knowledge*, published in 1958.

5. "Chapter II: The Method of Reflection" (typed).
The pagination suggests that HRN originally intended this item to be the second chapter in the manuscript "On Faith," listed above as item 4. The chapter is unfinished and bears the author's annotation "omit." The hypothesis that it was removed from "On Faith" explains at least partly why the remaining chapters in "On Faith" are variously numbered.

INDEX

"Present as the Locus of Reality, The"
(Mead), 88n
Principles of Psychology (James), ix

Rationalism, 28
Rawlinson, A. E. J., 105n
Reason, 3–4
Reconstruction of faith, 83–101
Reflection, 23–30
 social nature of, 35
Reformation, 8–9
Ritschl, Albrecht, 109
Royce, Josiah, ix, 48–49, 51, 56n, 60
Russell, Bertrand, 2, 7, 70, 71–72
 faith defined by, 14

Santayana, George, 65n
Saving faith, 9–10
Schleiermacher, Friedrich, 26, 65,
 183n, 107n
Science
 faith in, 1, 39, 41–42
 Russell on, 7
 seeing as element in, 12
 Ayer on, 17
 as belief, 34
Scientific Outlook, The (Russell), 71–
 72
Scriptures, 114–18
Seeing, and believing, 12–16
Sense-experience, 13, 17

Shelley, Percy Bysshe, 70, 72
Sin, 77–82
Society
 as context for believing, 34–40
 as association, 54
 as spiritual community, 55
State, 52–53, 57
Subjectivism, 23–24, 25, 27–28

Taylor, A. E., 13n, 32, 46n
Tertullian, 15–16
Thomson, James, 69
Tolstoy, Leo, 3
Treason, 49, 53–54, 81–82, 111–12
Trinitarian doctrine, 17
Trust
 Luther on, 9
 conviction contrasted with, 31
 believing as, 32–33, 36, 39–40
 and fidelity, 49
Truth
 subjective and objective, 10
 conviction of, 31

University, 51–52, 59–60

Voluntarism, 19

Whorf, Benjamin Lee, 36–37
Works, faith and, 5–12